UNSEEN REALITIES

HEAVEN, HELL, ANGELS AND DEMONS

UNSEEN REALITIES

HEAVEN, HELL, ANGELS AND DEMONS

R. C. SPROUL

LIGONIER MINISTRIES
RENEW YOUR MIND

CHRISTIAN
FOCUS

© R. C. Sproul 2011

paperback ISBN 978-1-84550-682-7
epub ISBN 978-1-84550-989-7
mobi ISBN 978-1-84550-766-4

Published in 2011, reprinted in 2012, 2017 and 2020
by
Christian Focus Publications
Geanies House, Fearn
Ross-shire, IV20 1TW, Scotland
www.christianfocus.com
with
Ligonier Ministries
400 Technology Park,
Lake Mary, Florida 32746
www.ligonier.org

Cover design by Paul Lewis

Printed by
Bell and Bain, Glasgow

CONTENTS

Dr. R. C. Sproul (1939–2017) was the founder and chairman of Ligonier Ministries, an international Christian education ministry based in Lake Mary, Florida. He also served as senior minister of preaching and teaching at Saint Andrew's in Sanford, Florida, and as president of the Ligonier Academy of Biblical and Theological Studies.

During his distinguished academic career, Dr. Sproul helped train men for the ministry as a professor at several leading theological seminaries.

He wrote more than seventy books, including *The Holiness of God, Chosen by God, The Invisible Hand, Faith Alone, A Taste of Heaven, Truths We Confess, The Truth of the Cross*, and *The Prayer of the Lord*. He also served as general editor of *The Reformation Study Bible* and wrote several children's books, including *The Prince's Poison Cup*.

Preface

C. S. Lewis' *The Screwtape Letters* is a wonderfully creative little book that teaches Christian living by imagining how demons might wage war against it. It consists of a series of letters in which Screwtape, a senior demon, mentors and coaches Wormwood, a junior demon, as to how best to trip up his "patient," a new Christian. Ultimately, the effort fails, as the patient is killed during wartime and is taken to glory.

It is interesting to me that in his final letter, when he reproaches Wormwood for his failure, Screwtape recounts the patient's "escape" with special emphasis on what the unnamed Christian saw in the moments after his death. Lewis writes:

> How well I know what happened at the instant when they snatched him from you! There was a sudden clearing of his eyes (was there not?) as he saw you for the first time, and recognized the part you had had in him and knew that you had it no longer....

As he saw you, he also saw Them.... The [angels] are strange to mortal eyes, and yet they are not strange. He had no faintest conception till that very hour of how they would look, and even doubted their existence. But when he saw them he knew that he had always known them and realized what part each one of them had played at many an hour in his life when he had supposed himself alone, so that now he could say to them, one by one, not "Who *are* you?" but "So it was *you* all the time." ... He saw not only Them; he saw Him. This animal, this thing begotten in a bed, could look on Him. What is blinding, suffocating fire to you is now cool light to him, is clarity itself, and wears the form of a Man.

I believe Lewis' insistence that death will bring a sudden clearing of one's eyes is wholly biblical. Did not the apostle Paul tell us: "For now we see in a mirror, dimly, but then face to face. Now I know in part, but then I shall know just as I also am known" (1 Cor. 13:12)? I'm less sure, as Lewis postulates, that we will instantly see that we have been troubled by personal demons and guarded by specific angels, but I am convinced that we will know with certainty that these beings exist and that heaven and hell are real places, just as our faith in God's existence will be confirmed by the blessing of gazing upon Him face to face.

Most of us accept the biblical testimony that there is a God who rules in heaven and earth (though we don't always accept everything Scripture says about Him). However, we are much less certain about other spiritual truths, such as heaven and hell, angels and demons, and their prince, Satan. We are like Wormwood's patient, who, in Screwtape's words, "even doubted their existence" until death brought clear sight. Why do we struggle to accept these things? God is no less invisible to us, yet we believe in and worship Him. Moreover, we fully accept that such things as microbes and germs exist, even though we cannot see them with the naked eye. Our selectivity when it comes to what we believe troubles me, for heaven and hell, angels and demons are taught as realities in Scripture as much as is God Himself.

I believe that if we are to be consistent Christians, believing all of the Bible rather than portions of it, we must recognize that the supernatural places and beings described on its pages are real. There is an uncompromised supernaturalism at the heart of the Christian worldview, and we must not let the world's skepticism with regard to these things affect our belief systems. We must trust and affirm that there is much more to reality than meets the eye. We must declare with Hamlet, "There are more things in heaven and earth than are dreamed of in your philosophy, Horatio."

I hope this brief tour through the Bible's teachings in regard to heaven and hell, angels and demons, will bolster your faith in Scripture's teachings regarding the supernatural. May we stand fast on the firm foundation of the inspired writings of the prophets and the apostles, waiting with anticipation that day when our vision will clear. And as Horatio G. Spafford taught us in his great hymn "It Is Well with My Soul," may we sing, "O Lord, haste the day when the faith shall be sight."

R. C. Sproul
Lake Mary, Florida
November 2010

PART ONE

———

Heaven

1

Thinking of Home

When I was a seminary student, I was completely awed by one of my professors, Dr. John Gerstner. He was awe-inspiring in several ways, not least of which was his encyclopedic knowledge of theology and philosophy, as well as the acute mind that he brought to bear in the classroom. I also admired him greatly for his profound spiritual depth and godliness.

One day, after Dr. Gerstner had given a provocative lecture, I felt compelled to ask him, "What's heaven like?" He gave me a strange look, as if to say: "How am I supposed to know? I haven't been there." I was so impressed by Dr. Gerstner's spiritual depth and understanding that I almost expected to get an eyewitness report from him. He ended up giving me some reading material that proved helpful to my understanding.

I don't think there is anyone who hasn't wondered what heaven is like or who hasn't considered the even more fundamental question: Is there a heaven?

Christianity has been criticized loudly in modern times for being a so-called "pie-in-the-sky" religion. Karl Marx popularized the idea that religion is the opiate of the masses; his thesis was that religion was invented and used by the ruling classes to exploit and oppress the poor people of the world and to keep them from revolting. The promise of "pie in the sky" was designed to encourage them to be good workers and to obey their masters—their reward would be deferred to eternity.

But one cannot take Christianity seriously without seeing the central importance of the concept of heaven. There really is a "pie-in-the-sky" idea that is integral to the Bible, and especially to the New Testament, and I'm afraid we've lost our appetite for the delights God has stored up for His people in the future.

From time to time, pollsters have asked Christian people to name their favorite chapter in the New Testament. When polls like that appear, there always seem to be two chapters that come in first and second. The chapters that vie for the greatest popularity in the New Testament are 1 Corinthians 13, the great "love chapter," and John 14.

As John 14 begins, Jesus is speaking to His disciples in His last great discourse with them in the upper room on the night in which He was betrayed, the night before His execution. He says: "Let not your heart be troubled; you believe in God, believe also in Me. In My Father's house are many mansions; if it were not so, I would have told you" (vv. 1-2a).

Jesus begins this part of the discourse with an admonition, an imperative to His disciples. He tells them, "Do not allow your hearts to be distressed or disturbed." This is a call to trust and to faith. He then goes on to reason with them in a succinct but profound manner. Because these words are so comforting to us, we may too easily gloss over the cogency of the argument that is contained in this brief exercise in reason.

Jesus says, "Let not your heart be troubled," and then He makes an assertion about the disciples. He says, "You believe in God." He doesn't ask them, "Do you believe in God?": He knows that they do. That's His first premise. He goes on to say, "Believe also in Me." This is central to the testimony of the New Testament—it is God who certifies and verifies the identity of Jesus. By endowing Christ with miraculous power and raising Him from the dead, God certifies that this is His beloved Son. Three times in the New Testament it is recorded that God speaks audibly from heaven, and on all three occasions the announcement is substantially the same: "This is my beloved Son." In one case, the voice says, "in whom I am well pleased." Another time it says, "Hear Him." Jesus is telling His disciples that God the Father both sent Him into the world and bears witness to His identity in the world; now, the night before He is to die, Jesus tells His disciples, "You believe in God; therefore, believe in Me."

Why does Jesus start with this premise, "You believe in God"? There's a real sense in which that proposition is the controlling idea for one's whole understanding of life, of the world, of death, and of heaven. If there is no God, there is no reason to have any significant hope for the continuity of personal existence that we call life; and yet, if God exists, what would be more ridiculous than to assume that He creates creatures in His own image who are destined to live as grass for a season, only to perish with all of their memories, all of their hopes, and all of their labor ending in meaninglessness?

We remember the line from Shakespeare's *Macbeth*: "Life's but a walking shadow, a poor player, that struts and frets his hour upon the stage, and then is heard no more." This refers, of course, to the life of the actor or the dramatist. What's the assessment? "It is a tale told by an idiot, full of sound and fury, signifying nothing." The image we get from that statement is that of a person who is in the limelight, in the spotlight, for a brief interlude of life, and then suddenly is silenced. The sentiment of this idea is that if this is the final conclusion to human existence, the story of life is an idiot's tale. An idiot is someone who is irrational, who doesn't make sense. An idiot is on the rim of madness, and the tales that he tells are not credible stories. They may be filled with sound and fury, with noise and passion. They may be loud and moving. But what do they signify? Nothing. I think the meaning of life is the great existential question that every human being faces at death.

I'll never forget the day that my son was born. I stood in the hospital and looked down at my firstborn son. I knew that my life was irrevocably changed. All relationships would now be different. I remember that occasion vividly because, when I went back to the hospital that evening, I took my mother to see her grandson. She was absolutely ecstatic about him, and when we got home, she said, "This is the happiest day of my life."

The next morning, I was awakened by my daughter calling to my mother. She came into my room and said, "Grandma won't wake up." As I walked into my mother's room, I realized that she was dead; she had died in her sleep. It was one of those weird, uncanny moments of human experience. It seemed to me that just moments before I had heard my mother say to me, "This is the happiest day of my life." She was a living, breathing, caring, passionate human being. Now she was lying lifeless in her bed. The previous morning, I had seen the newness of life with the birth of my son. On the same day that my son was born, my mother died. So I had an experience of the conflict between life and death. As I stood there, I said: "This doesn't make sense. Death doesn't make sense." Every fiber in my being said to me, "This cannot be the final conclusion for human experience."

My response could be explained away as an emotional need in my soul to believe that life is meaningful, but I was thinking in these terms: "If God exists, this cannot be the end." That's what Jesus is saying to His disciples when He says, "Let not your heart be troubled." When I stood beside my mother in that room, my heart was troubled—deeply troubled. But Jesus says: "Don't allow that. Let not your heart be troubled. If you believe in God, believe also in Me." And immediately upon making this connection between faith in the Father and faith in Him, Jesus says, "In My Father's house are many mansions; if it were not so, I would have told you." Do you hear what Jesus is saying to His disciples? As He approaches the moment of His death, He says to them: "Trust me. Trust the Father. He has a huge house with many mansions in it." And He says, "If this were not so, if this were just fantasy, if this were just emotional wish projection, if this were a fairytale or human superstition, I would have told you that."

Keep in mind that if Jesus Christ is God incarnate, He is the greatest theologian who ever walked the planet. He doesn't make theological mistakes, nor does He approve of theological error. He would not allow His disciples to go through the rest of their lives holding to a belief that was false. He says: "Your hope for life after death is not groundless. It is not a false hope. If it were a false hope, I would have told you. I would have corrected it."

He then goes on to say: "I go to prepare a place for you. And if I go and prepare a place for you, I will come again and receive you to Myself; that where I am, there you may be also" (vv. 2b-3). Jesus says: "I'm going home. I'm going to My Father's house. I'm going to receive My final inheritance, but I'm not going to heaven alone. I am going there to prepare a place for you so that where I am, you may be also."

Everyone, Christian or not, longs for reunion with those loved ones who have gone on before them, but the Christian longs to be with Christ. I cannot wait to see my father, my mother, and my friends who have died when I get to heaven, but the ultimate hope of my soul is to see the resurrected Christ in His Father's house, and He also has promised that that will happen.

How often have you wondered whether there is life after death? Sometimes we shrink in terror and in doubt when we contemplate something as wonderful as heaven purports to be. We sometimes are assaulted by the idea that it's just too good to be true. A few years ago, my wife and I were involved in a train accident in Alabama that killed more people than all the rest of the accidents in the history of Amtrak. Afterward, we had newspaper reporters poking microphones in our faces and asking questions like, "Why were you so lucky as to survive this?" and, "Why would God allow you to survive while He took other people's lives?" I've often thought about that experience, and one of the things that pops into my mind is the assumption behind those questions: the idea that I was the lucky one because I survived the train wreck. But if I hadn't survived it, I'd be home. I would be in heaven. We naturally cling to life in this world, fearful that what lies beyond is worse. But for those who are going to heaven, the bliss that God has stored up for them is unworthy to be compared with any joy or any delight we may cling to in this life.

2

Sitting on a Suitcase

I think every person who has ever been married has a humorous story to tell about his or her honeymoon, and I have one, too. It wasn't funny to me at the time, because my wife and I had gone together for eight years and had waited patiently for the day of our wedding. But all those years of waiting had not prepared us for how long the day of our wedding would be.

The afternoon wedding finally occurred on June 11, 1960, in Pittsburgh. After the wedding came an interminably long wedding reception, during which I shook hands with every person in the world, or so it seemed. Then came another reception at a relative's home, and then a long drive to the airport. We finally boarded a flight for New York City. We were planning to spend the night there at a hotel and fly out the next morning for the destination of our honeymoon, Bermuda.

We were excited about going to Bermuda. In preparation for our honeymoon, we had looked at all of the pictures and read all of the brochures, and had imagined the enchantment that awaited us once we arrived. I could think of no more enchanting place in all the world to go than Bermuda.

Our flight was supposed to take us to Kennedy International Airport in New York, but we had to land instead at the Newark airport. Our hotel, of course, was at Kennedy; we were to fly from there to Bermuda in the morning. I found a cab driver at the airport in Newark and asked, "How long will it take us to get over to Kennedy Airport?" He said, "In this traffic, it will take an hour to an hour and a half." I said, "No way am I going to do that." So I went back into the airport and hired a private plane, a little three-passenger thing to fly us from Newark to Kennedy. That was an adventure. The plane flew low over the skyline of New York, in between buildings and by the Empire State Building. In just a few moments, we were at Kennedy Airport.

The next step was to get from the airport terminal to the hotel. The pilot of the little plane told me, "When we land, go inside the terminal building. They have courtesy phones on the wall, and you can call the hotel where you're staying and they'll send a limousine to pick you up." So that's what we did. When I called the hotel, the receptionist said: "Yes, we have your reservation, Mr Sproul. We'll be right over to pick you up." Vesta and I went to the front of the terminal and sat down on our suitcases to wait. We sat there for an hour and a half, waiting on our wedding night for a limousine that never came. It took me that long to realize that they had forgotten us. When I called back, I learned they had picked up some other people, thinking they were Vesta and me. We sat there on our suitcases on our wedding night for an hour and a half.

Now here's my question: What would you think of us if I had said to Vesta, "We're having so much fun sitting here on our suitcases that I think we'll forget about our trip to Bermuda and cancel it"? You would think I had lost my mind. Yet that is the way we behave with respect to heaven. Jonathan Edwards once made the comment that no person who seeks to go on a pilgrimage to a glorious and exotic place will take up permanent residence at an inn along the way. It's nice to have a resting place, but we're always moving toward that which is better. Edwards said that Christians who cling tenaciously to this world and to this life are like sojourners who get stuck in a wayside inn, having lost sight of their glorious destination. We're headed for a place far more glorious than Bermuda. We're headed for heaven, and we need to understand not only that there is a heaven but that it is vastly superior to anything we experience in this world.

When the apostle Paul wrote the Philippian church, he was in prison and nearing the end of his life. The letter indicates that he's struggling with the circumstances in which he finds himself. He makes this statement: "For I know that this will turn out for my deliverance through your prayer and the supply of the Spirit of Jesus Christ, according to my earnest expectation and hope that in nothing I shall be ashamed, but with all boldness, as always, so now also Christ will be magnified in my body, whether by life or by death" (1:19-20). Do you hear what Paul is saying? "I don't know what they're going to do with me. They may cut my body to pieces. They may chop off my head. But whether I live or whether I die, Christ is going to be magnified and honored in my body, and I can say that with boldness."

How could he face this kind of circumstance with such confidence and such serenity of heart and spirit? The apostle writes, "For to me, to live is Christ, and to die is gain" (v. 21). Paul had one idea, one consuming passion: Christ. He was so focused on Christ that he said, "For me, to live is Christ. That's what I'm caught up in." But what's the next part of the statement? "And to die is gain." Paul is saying: "I enjoy fellowship with Christ right now. If I am alive, I am in Christ. For me to live is to enjoy fellowship with Christ, and if I die, it's gain." Now *gain* is an antonym for the word *loss*. We have a tendency to look at death as not only a loss but the worst of all possible losses. It is a loss for us when we lose loved ones to death, but is it necessarily a loss for them? Not if they're destined for heaven.

Let's see what else Paul says: "But if I live on in the flesh, this will mean fruit from my labor; yet what I shall choose I cannot tell. For I am hard-pressed between the two, having a desire to depart and be with Christ, which is far better. Nevertheless, to remain in the flesh is more needful for you. And being confident of this, I know that I shall remain and continue with you all for your progress and joy of faith, that your rejoicing for me may be more abundant in Jesus Christ by my coming to you again" (vv. 22-26).

From the record of history, it seems that Paul did survive this period of incarceration—this was not his final imprisonment—and that there was an extension of his earthly ministry so that he could fulfill the idea that he announced to the Philippians. But do you see the dilemma he expresses? "I'm in a strait between two things. I'm betwixt and between." He is experiencing a profound sense of ambivalence, a struggle within his heart in terms of his desires. On the one hand, he sees that it is pressingly urgent that he continue to live for the sake of his children in the faith. He wants to be of service to them. He knows that they need him, and he says, "I'm in a strait between these two things: whether to stay and be with you, which is far more needful, or to depart and be with Christ." It's as if Paul is saying: "I love being with you folks. You're my children in the faith. You're my friends. You're my beloved, but when it comes to being with you or being with Christ, there's no contest. So I'm torn between staying with you and leaving to depart and to be with Christ."

Then he gives a little parenthesis: "Which is far better." To live is Christ; to die is gain. Paul doesn't just say that the difference is between the good and the better, nor does he say that the difference is between the good and the best; the difference is between what is good and what is *far* better. The best is still beyond heaven, with the final consummation, with the resurrection of the body and so on, but the evaluation of the apostle is that the state we enter at death is not only a better situation than anything we enjoy in this world, it is *far better*. What would it do to our lives and to our confidence and to the health of our souls if we really believed that?

A few years ago, I was preparing to make a trip to speak at a conference. Everything was scheduled. People had registered for the conference. There was no way I could arbitrarily cancel my presence there. However, the night before I was to leave, I received a phone call that informed me that my beloved mentor, Dr. John

Gerstner, had collapsed in Pittsburgh while delivering a series of messages. I was told that he had had three strokes and that he was comatose and was not expected to live. I was shaken to my boots. Dr. Gerstner was elderly, and he had had close encounters with death before, so I had anticipated that at some point he would go home. I had wondered how I would feel when word came to me that my mentor had died. I knew I would feel like a spiritual orphan. I would feel vulnerable. I would feel alone. I would feel threatened to not have his stabilizing influence in my life anymore, just as a son feels when his father is taken from him.

So I was very concerned in my soul, and I thought, first of all, of mundane things. I wondered how in the world I could rearrange my schedule to go to this conference and get to the funeral in time if he should die in the next forty-eight hours. Then I began to think about how costly this would be for my life and my soul to be without my mentor, and then finally, through the grace of God, I began to think of what it would mean for him, and I thought: "If Dr. Gerstner goes home now, this afternoon, my guess is tonight he'll be sitting at a table, talking theology with Martin Luther, John Calvin, Augustine, and Jonathan Edwards, and for the first time in his entire life he will be having a theological conversation with peers, because he's never had that privilege in this world." And I thought, "What a glorious thing it will be for him when he crosses the threshold and enters into the heavenly sanctuary." This was a man whose indefatigable energy shamed all of us. If I had to speak four times in a single day, I would be spent and exhausted. After I was finished, I wouldn't be able to do anything productive for the rest of the day, and yet I had seen Dr. Gerstner, when he was seventy-five years old, stand in front of a camera and deliver twelve consecutive lectures and then say, "Would you like more?" He was tireless and relentless day in and day out. It occurred to me how weary he must be, and for him to enter into his rest, into the presence of Christ, would be far better for him. In that episode I was experiencing the struggle not for myself, about my own life, but about his life, the same struggle Paul was experiencing.

We know the answer to his struggle. Christ said to Paul: "Not yet, Paul. You still have more work to do. The hour will come when you can come home. I've prepared a place for you, but right now your place is in the ministry, working on behalf of the people."

So for a period of time, Paul had to experience what the Old Testament saints experienced. In Hebrews 11, the great faith chapter of the Bible, we read: "These all died in faith, not having received the promises, but having seen them afar off were assured of them, embraced them, and confessed that they were strangers and pilgrims on the earth. For those who say such things declare plainly that they seek a homeland. And truly if they had called to mind that country from which they had come out, they would have had opportunity to return. But now they desire a better, that is, a heavenly country. Therefore God is not ashamed to be called their God, for He has prepared a city for them" (vv. 13-16). The saints of the Old Testament looked beyond the grave, even as Job, in the midst of his torment and suffering said, "I know that my Redeemer lives, and He shall stand at last on the earth; and after my skin is destroyed, this I know, that in my flesh I shall see God" (19:25-26). The Old Testament patriarchs did not have the benefit of the historic record of the resurrection of Christ or of the words of Jesus, as we are able to study them today. They had vague, shadowy hopes and the promises of God, but on the basis of that, they withstood unimaginable torture, persecution, hatred, pain and suffering, because they sought a better country, a heavenly country, and they sought a city prepared by God. They did this because they understood that to depart and enter into heaven is *far better*.

I mentioned above the episode of Dr. Gerstner's collapse in Pittsburgh. The bulletin the next day was radically different. He woke up, and two days later he went home. A few weeks later he resumed his ministry, and he had to endure the same kind of delay that the apostle Paul experienced; he had to wait longer to enter into his rest.

I can remember talking with my grandmother when she was eighty-eight years old. A little tear formed in the corner of her eye, and she looked at me wistfully, and said: "I just don't understand why God won't take me home. I want to go." She was experiencing what Søren Kirkegaard said is one of the worst pains that we are ever called to endure: to want to die and not be allowed. To want to die in order to be free from pain is one thing, but to want to pass across the veil to see the face of Christ is something else. Have you come to the place in your thinking where you understand that death is not tragic for the Christian, but that it is a triumph—that it means crossing the threshold into glory?

3

Rising from the Dust

I mentioned in chapter one that on one occasion as a seminary student I asked my professor what heaven is like. It was a naïve question, because we don't have any information from pilgrims who have gone to that foreign country and have come back to give us a detailed description of what they've found. People ask me all the time, "Will I know my parents?" "Will I know my wife?" "Will we be recognizable?" "How old will we be in heaven?" "If we die when we are ninety, will we stay aged forever?" and "Will children who die be young forever?" All these questions assault us as we try to comprehend and conceive what heaven will be like. When people ask me such questions, I have to say that I don't know the answers.

One very popular question has to do with Jesus' statement that "In the resurrection they neither marry nor are given in marriage, but are like angels of God in heaven" (Matt. 22:30). People wonder, "What did

Jesus mean when He said that?" This statement from Jesus has provoked all kinds of speculation. I've read books that say that when we're in heaven we're going to be sexless because angels are sexless. But the Bible doesn't say that angels are sexless, and it certainly doesn't say that we will lose our gender identity when we go to heaven. Jesus simply says there will be no marrying and giving in marriage. That comes as a disappointment to people who would like to stay married to their spouses forever. Does Jesus mean that death ends the intimacy that is enjoyed by husbands and wives, that that relationship is abolished? I don't know.

The phrase "marrying and giving in marriage" is used in the Bible in the description of the expansion of wickedness that reached its zenith in the days of Noah, when people were doing what was right in their own eyes and were filling the world with violence. Jesus says, "In the days before the flood, they were eating and drinking, marrying and giving in marriage, until the day that Noah entered the ark" (Matt. 24:38). The idea is that life at the coming of Christ will be like it was in the days of Noah, when people were marrying and giving in marriage.

This statement by Jesus could be understood in at least two ways. First, it may refer to the suddenness of the appearance of divine judgment. He may be describing a situation in which people are going about the normal activities that characterize life as we know it, such as marrying and giving in marriage. In that case, all Jesus means to say is that His appearance will be unexpected.

Second, there's a theory that I can't confirm, but which I find fascinating and interesting. It is the idea that the phrase "marrying and giving in marriage" was a Jewish idiomatic expression for a low view of the sanctity of marriage in a degenerate culture where there was no sense of permanency to marriage. In other words, it was a situation in which people were getting married, quickly divorcing, then marrying again, time after time, and that was characteristic of the decadence of the age of Noah, which provoked God to bring the flood. Thus, it could be that Jesus is saying here that when we get to heaven, we're not going to have this cycle, this facile pace of marrying and giving in marriage. Maybe that's what He meant. I don't know.

The statement that there will be no marriage in heaven prompts us to ask, "Does that mean that the joy that accompanies the relationship of intimacy that God have given us in this world is over?" Here is my speculation, which has no foundation whatsoever in anything that's said specifically in Scripture. What if, in heaven, we are so sanctified that we can enjoy an in-depth, intimate, personal relationship with every other inhabitant of heaven, one that exceeds in intimacy and in joy the most joyous, personal, intimate relationship we have now? I think there's sound reason to believe that such relationships will be possible in heaven, that we'll be able to relate as closely, as openly, and as warmly to a thousand others in heaven as we do to our spouses now. In fact, once sin has been removed, we'll have a deeper personal relationship with people that we don't even know now than any relationship we enjoy in this world, because when we are glorified as human beings, all of the barriers to deep, personal relationships and communication that are put there because of sin will be gone. Maybe that's the secret Jesus is hinting at when He says there will be no marriage or giving in marriage in heaven.

We're not the first to ask such questions. The apostle Paul, in his first letter to the Corinthians, spent a good deal of time talking about the concept of heaven as it relates to the resurrection of Christ. In the fifteenth chapter of that letter, Paul gives a marvelous defense of the historical reality of the resurrection of Jesus and demonstrates that it is central to Christianity.

I realize that there are theologies today that seek to de-mythologize the New Testament and to retain the vestiges of Christianity without embracing the resurrection. I had a roommate in college who went into the ministry. When he had to go before the presbytery to be examined on his doctrine, he asked me: "Should I go with the resurrection of Christ or not? Should I tell the presbytery I believe that Christ was raised from the dead?" I asked, "What do you believe?" He said, "I don't think He was." I responded: "You're morally bound to say that you don't believe in the resurrection of Christ. You can't conceal that from the examining board of the presbytery." In the end, he did conceal it, and he was ordained. Ironically, a few years later I had to come before the same presbytery to be examined, and the examiner was that same man. He had to look me in the eye when he asked me whether I believed in the resurrection.

In any case, this was a major issue in the Corinthian church, and Paul gives a marvelous defense of the resurrection. He argues that if there is no resurrection, all kinds of things follow logically. But after he gives his defense of the truth of Christ's resurrection, he then answers two other questions: "But someone will say, 'How are the dead raised up? And with what body do they come?'" (v. 35). Who hasn't asked those questions?

Let me remind you that one of the most important lines found in the Apostles' Creed is the statement, "I believe in the resurrection of the body." This affirmation does not have to do with Christ's resurrection. To be sure, the apostles believed in the resurrection of Christ, but the creed here refers to our confidence that we will participate in the bodily resurrection of Christ. When we recite this affirmation, we're saying that we believe that our bodies will be raised from death and will be perfected, and that our bodies and souls will be reunited. That's what it means to say, "I believe in the resurrection of the body."

So Paul raises these questions: "How are the dead raised? And with what body do they come?" If you believe in the resurrection of the body, what are you talking about? Paul goes on to say, "Foolish one, what you sow is not made alive unless it dies. And what you sow, you do not sow that body that shall be, but mere grain—perhaps wheat or some other grain. But God gives it a body as He pleases, and to each seed its own body" (vv. 36-38). Here he borrows a statement almost verbatim from Plato and Socrates, an analogy drawn from nature. You plant a seed in the ground. Then you pour water on it, and you keep watering it and exposing it to the sunlight. Why do you do that? You do it because you're trying to cause the germination of life. You want that seed to produce a flower or a vegetable or grass. You want new life to come forth, so you water it. Does the water impart life to the seed?

No. The water kills the seed. It makes it rot, because the seed has to rot and die, as it were, before the germination takes place. It is like the metamorphosis of the caterpillar to the butterfly. The one has to be changed into the other. That's what Paul is saying. "What you sow is not made alive unless it dies. And what you sow, you do not sow that body that shall be." If we want grass, we don't throw grass in the dirt. We throw grass seed in the dirt. If we want flowers, we don't take the bloom from the flower and throw it on the ground and water it. You have to take seeds from the flowers and put them in the ground and water them.

When I was a child, my mother helped me plant a garden. We sent away for little packages of seeds for flowers and vegetables. She tediously showed me how we had to plant the seeds in straight rows and how to space the seeds so that there would be room for the mature plants to spread. After I had planted all of the seeds in the order that she told me to plant them, I had to take the packages that the seeds came in and put them on popsicle sticks like signs in the ground where I had put the seeds. That was so I would know where I had planted each kind of seed before the actual plants emerged. The best thing I produced in my gardening was seed packages on sticks. That was about the extent of my green thumb.

But Paul is pointing out something elementary and basic to life—that there are all kinds of bodies in the world, all kinds of living things, all kinds of grains, flowers, and vegetables. They all come from seeds, and different seeds produce different kinds of bodies. He says, "All flesh is not the same flesh, but there is one kind of flesh of men, another flesh of animals, another of fish, and another of birds" (v. 39). What else is there about bodies? "There are also celestial bodies and terrestrial bodies; but the glory of the celestial is one, and the glory of the terrestrial is another. There is one glory of the sun, another glory of the moon, and another glory of the stars; for one star differs from another star in glory" (vv. 40-41). Paul is saying, "Open your eyes to the wide diversity of reality that you experience—all sizes, shapes, forms, and structures of existing entities in the universe: stars and moons and trees and mountains and grass and waterfalls." If you just look at the animal kingdom, you'll see this myriad diversity of life. Do you think that in our experience we've seen every conceivable kind of life that there is and every conceivable kind of body there is? In our fantasies and science-fiction movies, the creative imaginations of the screenwriters produce all kinds of aliens that represent different kinds of life and different kinds of bodies. But Paul is saying, "There is a kind of body that no one has yet seen." Christ gave a foreshadowing of this when He came out of the tomb with the same body that He took into the tomb, with a body that had continuity with the one that was buried, but a body that had been changed. He had a glorified body, and Paul is saying here that there's a whole new dimension of life and of bodily existence for which we are being prepared.

Paul continues: "So also is the resurrection of the dead. The body is sown in corruption, it is raised in incorruption" (v. 42). He's not just talking about sin here, but about perishability. The body that I have now is getting old and weak; it's decaying; it's undergoing a kind of loss of strength and vitality. I long for a new body. My next body will be incorruptible. It will be invincible. It won't age. It won't decay. It won't wear out. It won't rot. It won't break. It won't get sick. Paul adds: "It is sown in dishonor, it is raised in glory. It is sown in weakness, it is raised in power. It is sown a natural body, it is raised a spiritual body. There is a natural body, and there is a spiritual body. And so it is written, 'The first man Adam became a living being.' The last Adam became a life-giving spirit.... As was the man of dust, so also are those who are made of dust; and as is the heavenly Man, so also are those who are heavenly" (vv. 43-45, 48). He concludes with this—think of it: "And as we have borne the image of the man of dust, we shall also bear the image of the heavenly Man" (v. 49). We will have bodies like the body of Christ.

We've asked the question, "When we get to heaven, will we be able to recognize people who are there?" Certainly their outward appearances will have changed, and we're accustomed to recognizing people strictly on the basis of outward appearances. I like to play around with oil paints. I'm a novice at it, but I once undertook to paint a portrait of Martin Luther. I had to do it in stages. The first stage was a very rough outline, where I tried to get the proportion of the head right and get the ear lined up with the nose and so on. I spent one night working on the easel and just roughing in the basic proportions of the portrait of Luther. When I had finished and cleaned up my paints and walked away, I stood back and looked at the painting from about thirty feet away. I said to my wife: "Vesta, look at that. If someone else was painting that portrait, and I came in and saw it from here in its raw and unfinished state, I would instantly know that that was a portrait of Martin Luther." That's not a testimony to my artistic ability. I'm merely saying that even though it was so incomplete and so unlike an exact replica of Luther's face, there was something on that canvas that I could recognize. In the same way, Jesus' body was different when He came out of the tomb. It was so different that people did not immediately recognize Him. But there were times when, with a second glance, they could see that it was Jesus. Your departed friends and relatives, when you see them in heaven, will appear different than they did in this life, but when you see them, you will know them, and they will know you.

4

No More Tears

The expectation among many Christians is that heaven, ultimately, will be somewhat ethereal and spiritual, that the world in which we live will be completely destroyed and that we will live in a vaporous place in the sky. But the New Testament does not teach the ultimate destruction of this world; rather, the New Testament speaks of the renovation of this fallen planet. Paul tells us in Romans, for example, that "the whole creation groans and labors with birth pangs" (8:22), and that at the consummation of the kingdom of God, in the final eschatological triumph of Christ, this world will go through a radical purging by which it will be renewed, not destroyed. The expectation of the New Testament, ultimately, is that heaven will be here after the earth has been transformed.

In the final two chapters of the book of Revelation, we find imagery that speaks of this in beautiful terms. Here we read of John's vision of the new heaven and of the new earth, and of the heavenly city, the New Jerusalem, that descends from heaven to the earth. This is the most vivid and graphic description of what heaven is like in all of Scripture. It is communicated to us through what is called apocalyptic literature, and apocalyptic literature is known for its heavy use of rich images and symbols, so this passage sounds strange to us when we read some of the descriptions of streets of gold and gates of pearls and so on. But these images and symbols all point beyond themselves to profoundly important realities.

Revelation 21 opens with these words: "Now I saw a new heaven and a new earth, for the first heaven and the first earth had passed away. Also there was no more sea" (v. 1). It is fascinating to me that the first statement about the new heaven and new earth is negative. It speaks of the absence of the ocean. There is no sea. That might come as a tremendous disappointment to those of you who have sand in your shoes and who love the beaches. For you, it may seem that a new heaven and a new earth without a sea would be a paradise without the necessary ingredients. However, for a Jewish person of the ancient world, this description was loaded with symbolic importance, because in Hebrew poetry the sea was the symbol of destruction. The sea was not the friend of the ancient Jews. Israel never developed a commercial sea trade. Rather, the sea was the place from which marauders came. The Israelites' archenemies and perennial enemies, the Philistines, controlled the coast. The shoreline was rocky and treacherous, and the terrible storms that swept in across the Mediterranean would stir up the lakes and bring the hot winds of the sirocco. All of these unpleasant things came off the sea, and so the sea was the image of destruction in the Jewish mind. We see this vividly in Psalm 46, where the psalmist speaks of how the sea roars and is troubled, how it beats against the mountains so that they are destroyed and cast into the midst of the waters.

The positive image in Hebrew poetry is the river, the well, or the spring—the River Jordan, for example, which cuts like a ribbon down the middle of the arid land of Israel, and is the source of life and nourishment. As we will see, in the New Jerusalem, there is a river of life that flows down the center of the city. So when we see the absence of the sea but the presence of the river, we are seeing symbols of the absence of destruction and the presence of life.

Then the apostle says, "I, John, saw the holy city, New Jerusalem, coming down out of heaven from God, prepared as a bride adorned for her husband. And I heard a loud voice from heaven saying, 'Behold, the tabernacle of God is with men, and He will dwell with them, and they shall be His people. God Himself will be with them and be their God" (vv. 2-3). Again, the imagery here is borrowed from the Old Testament, where the external, visible sign of God's promised presence with His people was the tabernacle. The tabernacle was pitched in the very center of the Israelite camp. The twelve tribes were situated almost like a clock, and in the very core, or hub, of that clock was the tabernacle, indicating that God was in the midst of His people. The tabernacle was called the "tent of meeting" because it was there that the people assembled to meet with God.

In the New Testament, Christ comes in the incarnation. John tells us, "In the beginning was the Word, and the Word was with God, and the Word was God" (John 1:1). A little later John says, "And the Word became flesh and dwelt among us" (v. 14a). The words that are translated "and dwelt among us" literally mean "tabernacled among us" or "pitched His tent in our midst," referring back to the symbolic presence of God in the tabernacle of the Old Testament.

What is this vision telling us? It is saying that in the consummation, God Himself shall be with His people. What we see here is a picture of the coming of the immediate presence of God in the midst of His people, and there's nothing more glorious about heaven than to be bathed in the radiance of the unveiled presence of God.

Then we read this: "And God will wipe away every tear from their eyes; there shall be no more death, nor sorrow, nor crying. There shall be no more pain, for the former things have passed away" (v. 4). When I was a little boy, I sometimes got into scrapes. There was a boy in our town who was something of a bully. He grew much faster than everyone else, so he towered over the rest of us, and he could be mean. One day, I was playing with some other kids, and this bigger boy began calling me bad names and making fun of me. He hurt my feelings, and I started to cry and went home. I can remember to this day walking into the kitchen. My mother was there cooking, and she had an apron on. When she saw I was crying, she rushed over and hugged me and asked me what was wrong. Through all my sobs I could hardly get it out, but she was very tender and calmed me down. Then she took the edge of her apron and wiped away my tears.

I remember that because I've seen it repeated many times in the drama of life. For instance, many years ago, I visited a friend in a Boston hospital. He was in the final hours of his life, and I remember being by his hospital bed, feeling utterly helpless because I couldn't do anything to help him except to take little pieces of ice and put them to his parched lips. As I was doing this on one occasion, he looked at me. He was too weak to speak, and a single tear formed in his eye. I took the little cloth that was on the bed stand and wiped away that tear. I don't know how to describe something like that—what is communicated from one human being to another when that kind of service is rendered, the drying away of a tear.

When my mother dried my tears, I experienced great consolation and comfort. My weeping stopped, and I was restored to a sense of equilibrium. But as my childhood went on, I cried again and again and again. However, John is telling us here that when God personally comes to His people and dries our tears, that will be the end of all crying due to pain, sorrow, grief, or unhappiness. In heaven, there will be a permanent cessation of these things. There will be no death, pain, or sorrow. All of the things that provoke us to weep will no longer be present. In fact, one of the most amazing things about this description of the nature of heaven is the emphasis on what is *not* in heaven. There is no sea. There is no death. There are no tears. There is no sickness. There is no pain. There is no sin. That's not an exhaustive list, as there are others things that we will see in this passage, but it's interesting to notice that the first thing that is announced is the end of suffering.

John continues:

> Then one of the seven angels who had the seven bowls filled with the seven last plagues came to me and talked with me, saying, "Come, I will show you the bride, the Lamb's wife." And he carried me away in the Spirit to a great and high mountain, and showed me the great city, the holy Jerusalem, descending out of heaven from God, having the glory of God. Her light was like a most precious stone, like a jasper stone, clear as crystal. Also she had a great and high wall with twelve gates, and twelve angels at the gates, and names written on them, which are the names of the twelve tribes of the children of Israel: three gates on the east, three gates on the north, three gates on the south, three gates on the west. Now the wall of the city had twelve foundations, and on them the names of the twelve apostles of the Lamb." (vv. 9-14)

This description speaks of the foundations and the walls of the New Jerusalem, and the number twelve figures prominently here. The multiples of twelve refer both to the twelve tribes of Israel, who are commemorated by the gates, and the twelve apostles of Christ, who are listed on the foundations. Remember, this is a city whose builder and maker is God, and the city of God rests on the foundation of the Old Testament prophets and the New Testament apostles, with Christ being the chief cornerstone.

The description goes on to point out several other things. The first is that the New Jerusalem is a perfect cube. John writes: "And he who talked with me had a gold reed to measure the city, its gates, and its wall. The city is laid out as a square; its length is as great as its breadth. And he measured the city with the reed: twelve thousand furlongs. Its length, breadth, and height are equal" (vv. 15-16). What does that call to mind? It reflects, or recapitulates, the dimensions of the earthly Holy of Holies, the innermost section of the earthly temple, which was also a perfect cube.

Verses 18-21 speak of the gorgeous jewels that adorn the city, and we read that the twelve gates are twelve pearls. Imagine that. You've heard popular references to "the pearly gates." Here they are. Each gate is a single pearl, translucent and magnificent. One can see through the doors into the interior courts, where the beauty of the light that floods the city is reflected and refracted from the facets of the jewels that adorn the city.

John says, "And the street of the city was pure gold, like transparent glass" (v. 21b). We do not think of gold as being transparent. In order for gold to be transparent, it has to be rolled out so that it becomes very thin. I wouldn't put it past God to create a place that literally looks like this. I will not be the least surprised to go to heaven and find myself walking down a street that is paved not with concrete, stone, or asphalt, but with gold in all of its beauty.

But then we read about some more things that are *not* there. John says, "But I saw no temple in it" (v. 22a). If there is one place where we would expect a temple, it would be in heaven. It's one thing to say there's no death, weeping, sorrow, sickness, or sea, but there also is no temple in heaven. The reason is obvious, isn't it? There's no need of a temple, because the temple symbolizes the presence of God with His people. When God is there in reality, visible to His people, there is no need for the earthly representation. John says just that: "For the Lord God Almighty and the Lamb are its temple" (v. 22b).

Also, "The city had no need of the sun or of the moon to shine in it, for the glory of God illuminated it. The Lamb is its light" (v. 23). That's another fantastic image—no sun. If there were a sun in heaven, we wouldn't be able to see it—it would be eclipsed, not by another heavenly body, but by the super-intensity of the radiance and refulgent glory of God Himself, which is so much more dazzling and so much brighter than any created thing such as the sun. The sun and moon are unnecessary there. The illumination of this city comes from the glory of God and of Christ.

Then we read in chapter 22:

> And he showed me a pure river of water of life, clear as crystal, proceeding from the throne of God and of the Lamb. In the middle of its street, and on either side of the river, was the tree of life, which bore twelve fruits, each tree yielding its fruit every month. The leaves of the tree were for the healing of the nations. And there shall be no more curse, but the throne of God and of the Lamb shall be in it, and His servants shall serve Him. They shall see His face, and His name shall be on their foreheads. There shall be no night there: They need no lamp nor light of the sun, for the Lord God gives them light. (vv. 1-5a)

What else is absent from the New Jerusalem? The curse of God, which means the wrath and judgment of God. And rather than darkness, which indicates the curse, the ultimate joy of heaven will be our experience of the beatific vision—the vision of the face of God unveiled. We who are there will look directly into the unveiled face of God, for we shall see Him as He is.

I encourage you to make time to sit down and read chapters 21 and 22 of the book of Revelation in their entirety, and think of these chapters as a letter from heaven, addressed to you to describe this place where Christ promised to go and prepare a room for you, if indeed you are in Him. We need to keep this vision of heaven in front of us at all times, for death will be completely swallowed up by the victory of the Lamb and of His kingdom. We need to keep that image before our eyes, so that no tear we shed in this vale of tears is wasted.

PART TWO

Hell

5

The Place of God's Disfavor

I suppose there is no topic in Christian theology more difficult to deal with, particularly on an emotional level, than the doctrine of hell. In fact, the doctrine has become so controversial in the modern era that it is almost never addressed.

Old-fashioned revival preaching was characterized by the idea of "hellfire and brimstone." This idea is especially connected with the Great Awakening in the eighteenth century and the ministry of Jonathan Edwards. No theologian or preacher is more associated with the concept of hell than Edwards. I once read a college textbook in which Edwards was used as an illustration of someone who was sadistic because he seemed to preach so often on the subject of hell. That bothered me, because while Edwards certainly believed in the reality of hell, he had a passionate concern for the spiritual well-being of the people in his congregation. The sadistic person takes some kind of delight or glee in contemplating another person's torment or torture, and that was certainly not true of Edwards. He preached on hell so his people would not have to experience it.

What a contrast from that time to our own. We seem to be allergic to any serious discussion of the doctrine of hell. In fact, there has probably never been a time in the history of the church when more people have challenged this doctrine than in our own day. Liberal theologians, of course, completely dismiss it as part of the mythological worldview of primitive people, a concept unworthy of the love of God and of Jesus. Others, even within the professing evangelical camp, have created quite a stir by suggesting the doctrine of annihilationism, which says that the ultimate judgment of the sinner is not ongoing, eternal punishment in a place called hell, but simply the annihilation of the person's existence, and that the great punishment, the great loss, that accompanies annihilation is the loss of the happiness promised to those who will live eternally in heaven. So we have moved away from looking very seriously at the concept of hell. People look back at Edwards and the frontier preachers as theologians who tried to scare people into the kingdom of God by holding out the threat of hell.

However, the concept of hell was not invented by Edwards, by John Wesley, or by any of the frontier revival preachers. Neither was it invented by the Reformers of the sixteenth century or by Thomas Aquinas or by Augustine. It is a biblical concept, and almost everything that we learn about hell in the Bible comes to us, oddly enough, from the lips of Jesus Himself. It is because Jesus spoke so frequently about hell that the church takes the concept so seriously, or at least *should* do so.

I remember my mentor, Dr. John Gerstner, giving a series of lectures on hell. In that series, Gerstner made this comment: "The idea of a hell that involves some kind of eternal punishment at the hands of a just and holy God is so profoundly difficult for us to handle emotionally, that the only person who would have enough authority to convince us of the reality of such a place would be Jesus Himself."

Whenever I enter into discussions about the doctrine of hell, people ask, "R. C., do you believe that the New Testament portrait of hell is to be interpreted literally?" When we look at some of the statements that are made about hell in the New Testament, we see that it is described in various ways—as a place of torment, as a pit or an abyss, as a place of eternal fire, and as a place of outer darkness. When people ask me whether these images of hell are to be interpreted literally, I usually respond by saying, "No, I don't interpret those images literally," and people typically respond with a sigh of relief.

One of the reasons that classical orthodox theology has tended not to interpret these images literally is because, if you do, you have a very difficult time making them agree with one another. If hell is a place of burning fire on the one hand and a place of outer darkness on the other hand, that's difficult to reconcile, because usually where there's fire, there's light. You can't have fire in a total darkness. So there is a collision of images there.

If we take the New Testament's descriptions of hell as symbolic language, we have to remember the function of symbols. The function of figurative language or metaphorical language in Scripture is to demonstrate a likeness to a reality. A symbol is not the reality itself. The symbol points beyond itself to something else. The question is whether the reality to which the symbol points is less intense or more intense than the symbol. The assumption is that there's always more to the reality than what is indicated by the symbol, which makes me think that, instead of taking comfort that these images of the New Testament may indeed be symbolic, we should be worrying that the reality toward which these symbols point is more ghastly than the symbols. I once heard a theologian say that a sinner in hell would do anything he could and give everything he had to be in a lake of fire rather than to be where he actually is. So even though we don't know exactly where hell is, how hell operates, and what it is really like, all of the imagery our Lord uses suggests that it is a place we don't want to go. It is a place of unspeakable pain and torment.

Again, the question is raised whether the punishment that people endure in hell is physical punishment, since the Scriptures speak about the resurrection of the body not only for the believer but also for the unbeliever, which means that a person in hell after the last judgment will be in a resurrected body suited for his punishment. Because so much of the language of hell in the New Testament refers to corporal punishment, many have drawn the conclusion that hell does indeed involve a relentless, endless, physical kind of suffering.

That may be the case, but other theologians have suggested that the essence of the punishment is in the torment of the soul, in being cut off from the blessedness of the presence of God and from His grace. Even to carry around that spiritual distress within a resurrected body would be torment enough. But, in the final analysis, these are issues about which we can only speculate.

Let's look for a moment at some of the passages in the New Testament that speak of this place called "hell." In Matthew 25, Jesus tells the parable of the talents, and toward the end of this chapter, Jesus says: "For to everyone who has, more will be given, and he will have abundance; but from him who does not have, even what he has will be taken away. And cast the unprofitable servant into the outer darkness. There will be weeping and gnashing of teeth" (vv. 29-30).

One of the questions people ask me is this: "Do you think that hell is separation from God?" I usually give a kind of enigmatic reply to that. First I say, "Yes, hell is a separation from God." Again, people breathe a sigh of relief when I say that. I think that when they hear me say that, they imagine that hell is simply a place where God is completely absent, not something terrible like a lake of fire. They imagine that it is just a place where people gather, such as in Jean-Paul Sartre's little play *No Exit*, where they're confined and condemned to a miserable existence dealing with each other, without the presence of God. But I then say, "Before you breathe a sigh of relief that hell represents the absence of God, let's think about that for a moment."

In the normal language of our culture, I see frequent allusions and references to hell. You've heard them. Someone comes back from a tour of duty in the military and uses the expression, "War is hell." Or someone who has endured great physical suffering says, "I went through hell in that experience." Those kinds of statements must be understood as hyperbole, that is, as obvious exaggeration. If we could find the person who is the most miserable person in the world today, the person who is experiencing suffering at the worst possible level, that person still is deriving certain benefits from the presence of God. God's graciousness, His benevolence, what we call His common grace, the grace that He gives to all people, is not totally removed from any individual during this lifetime. But in hell, it is removed. Being in a place where the blessings and the grace of God are utterly absent would be far worse than anything that could possibly befall us in this world. So, I don't take a lot of comfort in thinking that hell is the absence of God.

When someone asks me, "Is hell the absence of God?" I answer by saying "Yes" in the sense that it is the absence of God's benefits, the absence of His benevolence, His graciousness, and so on. But I think that if the people in hell could take a vote or have a referendum to deport one person from their midst, to expel one person from hell, I think that the universal vote would be given to God, because the person who is most unwelcome in hell is God Himself. As far as the people in hell are concerned, it would be wonderful if God would desert them altogether.

The problem with hell is not simply the absence of God's graciousness. It is the presence of God that is so difficult. God is present in hell because He is omnipresent. The psalmist declares, "Where can I go from Your Spirit? Or where can I flee from Your presence? If I ascend into heaven, You are there; If I make my bed in hell, behold, You are there" (Ps. 139:7-8). If God is everywhere in His being, then certainly He is in hell as much as He is anywhere else. The problem, then, is what He is doing there. He's there in His judgment. He is there in His punitive wrath. He is present in hell as the One who executes His justice on those who are there. That's why I say that anyone who is in hell would most want God, more than anyone else, to leave. This is our fundamental nature as sinners—to be fugitives from the presence of God. The very first sin provoked Adam and Eve to flee from the presence of God and hide themselves from Him. The last thing they wanted after they experienced guilt and shame was for God to be present. And that, if you can multiply it infinitely, is the experience of those who are in hell.

Jesus says that hell is the place of outer darkness. To understand the force of that, we have to think of it in light of the Old Testament imagery about the outer places and the outer darkness. We remember that God described two alternatives for those who received His law. To those who kept the law, He promised blessedness, and for those who renounced, rejected, or disobeyed His law, He promised His curse. The whole concept of curse in the Old Testament was articulated with the imagery of darkness, of an outer darkness, the darkness that was outside the commonwealth of Israel, outside the camp. Conversely, the presence of God was described as a place of light where the glory of God radiated all around. So when Jesus warns about the outer darkness, He's warning about the place of the curse, the place where the light and radiance of God's countenance does not shine.

Also in Matthew 25, Jesus says that those who will be cast into the outer darkness will experience "weeping and gnashing of teeth." This is a concrete image that any Jew would understand, and one I think we can all readily comprehend. There are different kinds of weeping. There is the weeping of those who mourn. There is the weeping of those who are in pain. And there is the weeping of those who are deliriously happy. But when we add to this notion of weeping the idea of gnashing of teeth, it is obvious that Jesus is not describing a pleasant circumstance. He is talking about a deep, mournful kind of wailing. But the gnashing of teeth, as we see in the New Testament, is often associated with hatred. When the crowd heard Stephen proclaim the Word of God, they gnashed their teeth in fury (Acts 7:54).

When a person spends time in hell, his relationship with God does not improve. The person goes to hell in the first place because he is hostile toward God. As he experiences the outer darkness where he weeps, he gnashes his teeth in ever-greater hatred of his Maker.

The nature of hell is not completely clear to us. That is why people often ask me questions about hell, questions to which I do not always have easy answers. However, because our Lord tells us so much of what we know about hell, I believe these questions are important ones.

6

The Great Separation

We have seen that much of what we know about hell comes to us from the lips of Jesus. One of Jesus' main teachings concerning the doctrine of hell is His parable of the sheep and the goats, found in Matthew 25. It reads:

> When the son of man comes in His glory, and all the holy angels with Him, then He will sit on the throne of His glory. All the nations will be gathered before Him, and He will separate them one from another, as a shepherd divides his sheep from the goats. And He will set the sheep on His right hand, but the goats on the left. Then the King will say to those on His right hand, "Come, you blessed of My Father, inherit the kingdom prepared for you from the foundation of the world: for I was hungry and you gave Me food; I was thirsty and you gave Me drink; I was a stranger and you took Me in; I was naked and you clothed Me; I was sick and you visited Me; I was in prison and you came to Me." Then the righteous will answer Him, saying, "Lord, when did we see You hungry and feed You, or thirsty and give You drink? When

did we see You a stranger and take You in, or naked and clothe You? Or when did we see You sick, or in prison, and come to You?" And the King will answer and say to them, "Assuredly, I say to you, inasmuch as you did it to one of the least of these My brethren, you did it to Me." Then He will also say to those on the left hand, "Depart from Me, you cursed, into the everlasting fire prepared for the devil and his angels: for I was hungry and you gave Me no food; I was thirsty and you gave Me no drink; I was a stranger and you did not take Me in, naked and you did not clothe Me, sick and in prison and you did not visit Me." (Matt. 25: 31-43)

In the previous chapter, we talked about some of the images of hell that Jesus uses in His parable of the talents. Here, in the parable of the sheep and the goats, Jesus uses another image—an image of separation. He talks about the King who will separate kingdoms and people just as a shepherd divides sheep from goats. The sheep refer to those who have been obedient, who have been followers of Christ; they will inherit the kingdom of heaven that was prepared for them from the foundation of the world. The goats, on the other hand, will be excluded from the presence of the company of God and His angels in heaven, and they will be sent away into everlasting fire.

What Jesus is describing here is the concept of judgment. It is interesting to me that the New Testament word for "judgment" is the Greek word *krisis*, from which we get the English word *crisis*. It comes directly over into our language from the Greek. The supreme crisis for humanity will be the crisis of the last judgment. That will be the time of separation.

Behind and beneath the New Testament concept of hell stand some other ideas that we must understand if this is to make sense to us. First of all, there is the concept of the justice of God. We say that God is just and that He judges according to His own holiness and perfect righteousness. God is the Governor of the universe. He rules over all people, and He holds every human being personally accountable to Himself. If Jesus Christ taught anything in His earthly ministry, it is that there will be a final judgment for human beings—that every one of us will be called into account before the presence of God, and we will be judged by His perfect righteousness and His perfect law.

When we look at the imagery the New Testament uses to describe the response of sinners to the charges leveled against them by the perfect and holy God at the last judgment, the primary image is that of silence. The New Testament says that every mouth will be stopped because there is nothing a person can say to defend himself against a judge who is perfectly just and omniscient. There's no reason to try to lie our way through the trial, because we can't fool our Creator; He has a perfect record of everything we have ever done, said, and even thought. As the Old Testament says about God, "There is not a word on my tongue, but behold, O LORD, You know it altogether" (Ps. 139:4). Jesus warns us, "For every idle word men may speak, they will give account of it in the day of judgment" (Matt. 12:36).

Think about that. God is going to hold us individually accountable not only for everything we've ever done, but for everything we've ever said—even casual remarks, off-hand statements, and idle words will be brought into the judgment. If our idle words are going to be brought into the judgment, how much more will those words that we speak with great seriousness come before His bar of justice. So we have to fear, first of all, a God who is just and holy. The author of Hebrews says, "How shall we escape if we neglect so great a salvation?" (Heb. 2:3a). Of course, he is saying that there *is* no escape. Then the warning is added that our God is a consuming fire (Heb. 12:29).

We don't like to think that we will be held accountable for our actions in this world. A man once said to me: "R. C., I've known lots of doctors. I once knew a doctor who was a coroner. He said to me that he had performed thousands of autopsies over his career and that he had never seen a soul." My friend thought he was being clever and profound. He was making this point: "I don't believe that there is a soul. I don't believe that there is personal survival beyond the grave, so I can eat, drink, and be merry without any fear of ultimate consequences." I asked, "Whatever made you think that a coroner or any other earthly instrument would be able to detect or discern something that is immaterial?"

Beyond that attitude, there is an almost universal assumption in American culture that if there is life after death, then everyone's going to go to the same place, to the eternal blessedness of heaven. Nothing turns a sinner into a saint faster than death. When we lay to rest the most reprobate person, we speak in glowing terms of confidence that he is enjoying felicity and peace in heaven, when, in fact, he may have just entered the gates of hell. But to contemplate his condition under that scenario is more than we can humanly bear. One of the reasons there is such a profound emotional and visceral response to the doctrine of hell is that it's difficult for anyone to contemplate another human being going there.

Even when it comes to the most despicable person I can think of, I can't enjoy the thought of his being in hell. Sometimes a movie will feature a villain who is utterly despicable. Perhaps the movie shows a little child sleeping in her bedroom at night, and then the camera shifts to the presence of a kidnapper sneaking into the house, coming up to the room, abducting the child, and then killing the child. Later, as he is about to make another attack on a child, the police are bearing down on him, trying to stop him. As you become involved in the movie, you are rooting for the police to get there in time to stop this person from committing another horrendous crime against a child. Finally, as the villain is about to kill the child, at the last second, a police officer shoots and kills the man. Then there is an audible response from the people in the theater. They cheer that the bad guy got his just desserts. But it's one thing for us to cheer the punishment of a sinner in this world. It's another thing to cheer the idea of any human being undergoing eternal, relentless punishment at the hands of God. So we turn away from such an idea out of a commitment to our basic humanity and our basic human concern about the wellbeing of others.

But what do we do with the emphatic teaching of Christ and of the other authors of the New Testament books, who insist there will be a judgment and a separation, that some people will enter heaven and others will be cast into that place of outer darkness where there will be weeping and gnashing of teeth?

I believe the most terrifying sermon ever preached was the Sermon on the Mount, because Jesus ends the sermon by warning the people that "Many will say to Me in that day, 'Lord, Lord, have we not prophesied in Your name, cast out demons in Your name, and done many wonders in Your name?' And then I will declare to them, 'I never knew you; depart from Me, you who practice lawlessness!'" (Matt. 7:22-23). Jesus says that there are some people whom He and the Father will reject on the occasion of the last judgment.

Furthermore, nothing in Scripture gives us the slightest hint that there will be a second chance after death, so the longer we postpone repenting of our sin and fleeing to Christ, the more perilous is our condition. Tonight our souls may be required of us (Luke 12:20). We can't assume that everyone is just simply going to walk peaceably into heaven and escape the judgment—not if we're to take the teaching of Jesus Himself seriously. He speaks of separation and of a crisis, the crisis of the judgment of God.

The final verses of Matthew 25 read this way: "Then they also will answer Him, saying, 'Lord, when did we see You hungry or thirsty or a stranger or naked or sick or in prison, and did not minister to You?' Then He will answer them, saying, 'Assuredly, I say to you, inasmuch as you did not do it to one of the least of these, you did not do it to Me.' And these will go away into everlasting punishment, but the righteous into eternal life" (Matt. 25:44-46).

I once spoke on Sunday morning to the national convention of the Christian Booksellers Association. There were about six thousand people in the hall, and I ventured to speak on the subject of salvation, asking the question, "What is salvation?" I thought I was taking a great risk. I thought: "I'm insulting these people's intelligence. I'm speaking here to the choir, as it were, to people who are involved in producing resources for Christian growth, and I'm talking about the most elementary concept there is in Christianity—the concept of salvation." Still, I wasn't completely sure that just because my hearers were involved in the business of Christian retailing that they all were trusting Christ for their eternal destinies. So I went ahead with my talk, and I posed this question to that congregation: "Since the Bible is always talking about salvation, from what are we being saved?" In the Bible, the term *saved* is used in many different contexts. If you're restored to health from a threatening illness, your life is saved. If an army escapes sure defeat in battle, they experience salvation. But the fundamental meaning of *saved* is to have escaped some calamity. So when we speak about ultimate salvation in the Scriptures, we're talking about an escape from the ultimate calamity. And what is that ultimate calamity? It is the wrath of God visited justly on those who have remained hostile to Him.

So I concluded my sermon at the booksellers' convention this way: "That from which you are saved ultimately is God." We like to think of God as the Savior, as the One who redeems us from judgment, and indeed, He is our Savior if we have genuinely repented and cast ourselves on the mercy of Christ. So God is the Author of salvation, and yet, to be saved, in the final analysis, is not simply to be saved *by* Him, but to be saved *from* Him, because the ultimate crisis, the worst calamity a person could ever face, is the judgment of a holy God.

It's not that we're afraid of being brought before a corrupt judge who might punish us beyond what we deserve. Rather, we fear being visited by a judge who is just, One who will judge us perfectly according to what we deserve, according to what we have earned, according to our merit. Of course, the Bible makes clear that the only merit we bring to the throne of God in the last judgment is de-merit. The only thing that we have earned at the hands of perfect justice is perfect punishment.

But we're at ease in Zion. Preachers aren't preaching hell. This message of Christ has been all but deleted from the New Testament in our day, and we say, "We don't have anything to worry about from God because God is so loving that He is going to save everyone." Well, if He is going to save everyone, it will not be without a serious rebuke against His only begotten Son for teaching falsely that there will be separation, that there will be curse as well as blessing, that there will be punishment as well as rewards, and that hell was created for the Devil, for his angels, and for all who willingly participate with them.

I used to train people for Evangelism Explosion, and we used two diagnostic questions to engage people in discussion. The first diagnostic question we used was this: "Have you come to the place in your spiritual life or in your thinking where you know for sure that when you die, you will go to heaven?" I've asked that question to literally hundreds and hundreds of people, and most of them answered by saying, "No, I'm not sure about that." Once, however, I got a particular response

I'll never forget. When I asked this question to one man, he looked me in the eye, and he was trembling. He wasn't being facetious and he wasn't trying to be a smart aleck. He said: "No. I know that I'm going to hell, and it scares me to death." He was on the road to hell. When I shared the gospel of Christ with him, he repented of his sins and became a Christian. But it was interesting to me that God had already begun to work in him, to convict him of his sin, and to give him a certain healthy fear for what would lie ahead in his existence if he did not repent. We all need to have that fear of the ultimate crisis of judgment that lies ahead for each of us.

7

Degrees of Punishment

One of the common objections to the doctrine of hell as it has been taught historically in orthodox Christianity is that this doctrine demeans the character of God, that it somehow casts a shadow over His goodness. People say to me: "My God is a God of love. And my God is a good God. Since God is really loving and good, He would never send anyone to hell." I hear this constantly, and I wonder about the logic of it. Let's look at the premises that lead to the conclusion that God would never send anyone to hell.

The first premise is that since God is really loving, He would never send anyone to hell. By analogy, a loving parent would never chasten or punish his child. You might say: "Well, wait a minute, R. C., the punishment that a loving parent gives to a child is corrective. It is a chastisement that is designed to help the child avoid further difficulties later in life." Certainly, the New Testament teaches that God chastens those whom He loves, and this chastening is given for our welfare. But when we're talking about hell, we're not talking about the manifestation of God's corrective wrath; we are talking about His punitive wrath, the wrath that is not designed simply for the moral improvement of those who receive it, but is an expression of God's justice. You might ask me, "If God is really loving, how can He visit punitive wrath on people?"

We have to ask ourselves this question: "What is the object of God's love?" The Bible does speak of the benevolence that God displays toward all mankind, a kind of love that He has for everyone, but let's not jump to the conclusion that God's benevolent love is unconditional and eternal to a fallen human race. I once heard a preacher on television say repeatedly, "God loves everyone unconditionally." I wondered where that preacher got that message. He certainly didn't get it from biblical sources, because God's salvific love is conditional. It requires repentance and faith on our part, and the work of Christ, as well. There is a divine benevolence that God gives indiscriminately to people who have not repented and not come to faith, but that does not extend forever, because there was a design for that lovingkindness—to give people opportunity to repent and to take advantage of the mercy that is offered in Jesus Christ.

In addition to God's love for us as sinful creatures, God has a greater love, and that is His love for righteousness and for His own character. God is not going to compromise His holiness or His righteousness in order to accommodate us. There is a sense in which God loves His own glory. And the punishment of recalcitrant, impenitent persons in hell redounds to the glory of God. That may be one of the most difficult concepts for us ever to grasp—that hell, in one sense, glorifies God. How can that be possible? In simple terms, hell glorifies God by showing, in clear terms, the goodness of God.

But wait—didn't I just say that two of the most frequent objections against hell are the claims that God is loving and good? People reason that if God is loving and good, there can be no hell. According to this perspective, God's goodness must demand that He be loving enough to save everyone, regardless of their response to Him. The concepts of God's love and God's goodness are very closely related here. The protest against hell is: "If there is a hell, God is not really loving. And if He's not really loving, He's not really good." So if we believe that God is good, then we believe that He is loving, and that there is no limit to that love, as there is no limit to His goodness. Therefore, if He is loving, and if He is good, no one will ever go to hell.

However, does a good judge, a just judge, leave evil unpunished? If the courts in this world were to refuse to bring judgment on those who are known to be guilty of gross and heinous crimes, would we say those courts were good? Of course not. So what is meant by the goodness of God?

A theologian friend of mine once served on a jury, and the foreman of the jury said, "We're not here to discern right and wrong, but to deal with human relationships." That's the mentality of our age. We sometimes think that God's central concern should be human relationships, not the punishment of evil. If God insists on punishing evil, He must not be good.

But I think the opposite is the case. Seen from another
perspective, God's punishment of wickedness actually
demonstrates His goodness. God would not be good
if He didn't punish the wicked. He would not be good
if He completely abandoned His righteousness or His
justice.

However, we sometimes rely on the opposite assumption—the idea that God's love will mitigate His
goodness. We are at ease in Zion because we are convinced—or at least we cross our fingers and hope—
that God will not be just, that God will not be good.
But it is precisely because God is good that there is
such a place as hell where He punishes evil.

We have already seen that Jesus discussed hell quite
frequently. Like Jesus, the apostle Paul did not hesitate to deal with the theme of a just judgment at the
hands of God. Like Jesus, Paul warns us to flee from
the wrath that is surely to come. In Paul's letter to the
Romans, we read: "Therefore, you are inexcusable,
O man, whoever you are who judge, for in whatever
you judge another you condemn yourself; for you who
judge practice the same things. But we know that the
judgment of God is according to truth against those
who practice such things. And do you think this,
O man, you who judge those practicing such things,
and doing the same, that you will escape the judgment
of God?" (2:1-3).

Paul is asking a question here: "Do you think, if you
are sinning, that you are going to escape the judgment
of God?" Of course, Paul is giving this teaching in the
second chapter of Romans in anticipation of unfolding
the gospel of forgiveness and of justification by the free
mercy of God. He's laying the foundation, building

the framework for us to understand the cross and the doctrine of justification, and he's saying that unless we have a Savior, we're in serious trouble. He's addressing people who think they don't need Christ, who think that they will escape the judgment of God.

Are you counting on that? Are you hoping that God will be merciful to you in spite of your refusal to embrace His Son? I find no reason for such hope anywhere in Scripture; the Bible never hints that God will be anything but relentless in His insistence that one must repent of his or her sins and come to Christ in order to escape hell. We remember that when Paul spoke to the philosophers on Mars Hill in Athens, the cultural center of the ancient world, he spoke of the patience of God, and he said: "Truly, these times of ignorance God overlooked, but now commands all men everywhere to repent, because He has appointed a day on which he will judge the world in righteousness by the Man whom He has ordained. He has given assurance of this to all by raising Him from the dead" (Acts 17:30-31). Do you hear what Paul is saying? Repentance isn't an option. Paul does not speak in the style of an evangelist who says, "All you have to do is walk down the aisle, raise your hand, or recite this prayer after me." God doesn't invite people to be saved. He commands them.

What happens if we disobey this command? God commands us to repent. But we are complacent, saying: "I'm not going to repent. I'm not going to embrace Christ because I don't have to worry about it. There won't be any consequences for my sin." Most of the world is doing exactly what Paul is warning against here. They are thinking that they will escape the judgment of God. They can go hear preacher after preacher and listen to theologian after theologian who will give them all the security they desire, reinforcing their hope that God is not going to judge them. And they'll do it by denying the very reality of hell.

Paul goes on:

> Or do you despise the riches of His goodness, forbearance, and longsuffering, not knowing that the goodness of God leads you to repentance? But in accordance with your hardness and your impenitent heart you are treasuring up for yourself wrath in the day of wrath and revelation of the righteous judgment of God, who "will render to each one according to his deeds": eternal life to those who by patient continuance in doing good seek for glory, honor, and immortality; but to those who are self-seeking and do not obey the truth, but obey unrighteousness— indignation and wrath, tribulation and anguish, on every soul of man who does evil. (Rom. 2:4-9a)

This is a scary passage, because what Paul is describing here is a hoarder. When we used to play Monopoly at home, my daughter would rebuke my son for hoarding. He would stash away some of his money so the rest of us wouldn't know how much he had in reserve. But my daughter was quick to discern this ploy. She would look at him and say, "You're hoarding." Well, the idea behind hoarding is to amass a reserve supply of something against a rainy day. Paul says here that those of us who neglect the goodness and the patience of God, who assume we're going to escape His judgment apart from relying on Christ, are treasuring up or storing up wrath in the day of wrath.

I remember being in charge of an ordination exam for a man who was coming into a church as a minister. During that examination, I asked him whether he believed in the degrees of guilt. He emphatically responded in the negative. He said: "No, everyone is equally guilty. All sin is equally heinous. James says, 'If you sin against one point of the law, you sin against the whole law.'" The man who was being examined had made an illegitimate inference from that text to conclude that all sin is equal. He denied that there are different levels in heaven or gradations of felicity there, or levels to hell, as Dante imagined in his famous *Inferno*. But here in Romans 2, Paul is talking about hoarding judgment, amassing wrath, heaping it up, piling it up. Every time we sin, every day that we delay repenting of our sin and coming to faith in Christ, we are adding to our guilt before God, and thereby adding to our punishment in hell.

Remember, in His perfect justice, God punishes each sin justly. If someone is guilty of five counts of murder and someone else is guilty of but one count of murder, the punishment that God gives in His final courtroom will be perfectly just. The person who has committed five murders will be judged five times worse than the one who has committed one murder. We don't have the ability to do that in this world, but God does. This is the sober warning of the apostle, that we are building a case against ourselves. The longer we sin without repentance and without fleeing to Christ, the worse our judgment will be.

Jesus Himself teaches this concept repeatedly. He speaks of the unprofitable steward (Luke 16:1-8), and He talks about those who will be beaten with few stripes and those who will be beaten with many stripes (Luke 12:47-48). He talks about the judgment that will fall on Bethsaida as being greater than the judgment that will go to Sodom and Gomorrah, or Tyre and Sidon (Matt. 11:22). There will be various degrees of punishment because hell is the place where perfect justice is exacted. Though we are all guilty and all deserve to go to hell, still there are degrees and gradations of guilt of those who go there. Just as the rewards in heaven will differ according to the level of obedience we offer to Christ during our lifetime, so the punitive wrath of God will differ in intensity according to one's light and opportunity.

Do you see the problem that we have with hell? In the first instance, we deny it. Then, if we affirm it or think it might possibly be true, we neutralize it by saying that everyone is in the same boat and receives the same punishment.

I don't want to be in the most wonderful level of hell. I don't want to be there at all. Though there are degrees of reward and felicity in heaven, and degrees of punishment in hell, the gap between the two places is almost infinite. It's a huge, unbridgeable chasm. But we have to understand our peril in taking for granted the mercy of God and tempting Him, assuming that He is incapable of bringing us to justice or unwilling to do so. Beloved, He will bring me to justice, and He will bring you to justice. And when we are brought to that tribunal, if we're given the righteousness of Christ for our justification, we will escape His wrath, but if we abandon, avoid, or neglect Christ, we will be brought to justice alone.

8

The Point of No Return

The parable of the rich man and Lazarus is significant to any discussion of the concept of hell. We find it in Luke 16, where we read:

> There was a certain rich man who was clothed in purple and fine linen and fared sumptuously every day. But there was a certain beggar named Lazarus, full of sores, who was laid at his gate, desiring to be fed with the crumbs which fell from the rich man's table. Moreover the dogs came and licked his sores. So it was that the beggar died, and was carried by the angels to Abraham's bosom. The rich man also died and was buried. And being in torments in Hades, he lifted up his eyes and saw Abraham afar off, and Lazarus in his bosom. (vv. 19-23)

This isn't the end of the parable, but I want to pause at this point to make some preliminary comments on what we have read so far. The general rule of interpretation for parables is that we should look, basically, for one central point. This is not always the case. For instance, the parable of the sower makes several significant points in virtually allegorical fashion. But in general, it is misguided to try to find a one-to-one correspondence in meaning for each individual detail in an analogy, illustration, or anything resembling a parable. We can get lost in a sea of confusion if we do that with parables. That's why it's often very difficult to give a sound interpretation of a parable.

Having said that, I must add that we can rest assured that when Jesus borrows an illustration from nature or from the common life of the people, or comes up with a fictitious story to illustrate a point, though every point in the story may not carry with it a certain theological message, He would not make a statement that would be fundamentally incorrect. In other words, He would not use as part of His illustration some idea that would be in direct conflict with the teaching of the Word of God elsewhere. So that gives us a little bit of license to speculate in principle about some of the secondary ideas that are contained within the parable.

With that in mind, let's look at this opening segment of the parable of the rich man and Lazarus to get an idea of where Jesus is going. He begins by describing, and contrasting, two human beings, one who is fabulously wealthy and the other who is living in a miserable situation. This second man's experience is marked not only by abject poverty but also by relentless suffering. He is stricken and afflicted with sores, which dogs come to lick. We could look at that little detail in two ways. We can see his misery as exacerbated and intensified by the presence of the dogs, which were despised creatures in Israel; to be called a "dog" in Israel was to be insulted in the worst degree. So Jesus may be trying to emphasize this man's misery by saying that the dogs were coming to lick his sores. Others have argued that when a man has sores on his body, a dog will repeatedly lick at those sores to try to bring some relief or comfort. So maybe what Jesus is getting at here is that the only comfort this man received was not from kindly human beings but from dogs; the dogs were more concerned for his well-being than the rich man or anyone else. At least they had the grace to come and try to minimize his pain and suffering. In either case, however, the image is clear. This man is in a most miserable condition.

The description of the rich man includes the detail that he was clothed in purple and fine linen. A person reading this in the ancient world would have seen immediately that this person was living the lifestyle of a king. We remember that kings were garbed in purple. In fact, to be elevated to the realm of the purple was to be elevated to the realm of the crown. So this man's riches are described by Jesus in the most elegant terms, because only those with fabulous wealth could afford garments that were dyed in purple and spun from fine linen. Obviously, Jesus is trying to paint a picture of extreme contrast between fabulous wealth and terrible poverty.

This might incline us to think that the main point Jesus is trying to communicate in the parable is that all poor people go to heaven and all rich people go to hell. But we must not draw that conclusion from this parable, because such a teaching would be on a collision course with what the Scriptures say elsewhere. We know there are many examples in the Bible of people who were fabulously wealthy and at the same time profoundly godly. One who is mentioned in the parable itself—Abraham—was one of the wealthiest men of the ancient world. Joseph of Arimathea was another man of great wealth who was noted for allowing Jesus to be buried in his tomb. So the Bible doesn't say that anyone who is wealthy will ultimately go to hell and that it is intrinsically sinful to be wealthy. We don't want to draw that conclusion, although Jesus does frequently warn that those who have vast amounts of resources may have difficulty coming into the kingdom of God, for they have a tendency to think that they are self-sufficient. Jesus teaches this in the parable of the rich fool, who was so concerned about amassing wealth in this world that he neglected the care of his soul (Luke 12:16-21). But neither is Jesus teaching that all poor people go to heaven. The Bible denies both justification by wealth and justification by poverty. There's no particular inherent virtue in being poor, though it is often the poor people who flock to the comforts of Christ: because they find no comfort in this world, and no satisfaction in material things, they seem to be more open to hearing the message of the kingdom of God.

We're also told that the rich man fared sumptuously every day. His was a life of uninterrupted pleasure and hedonism. But Lazarus was laid at the rich man's gate each day, desiring to eat the crumbs that fell from the rich man's table. We remember the institution of gleaning in the Old Testament, in which God required land owners and farmers not to harvest and sell everything that they produced, but to leave the corners of the fields open for the poor to come and pick up what was left over from the harvest so that they would not be utterly destitute. You may see street people today who, in a pathetic expression of poverty, walk around with bags that contain everything that they own, or they may even push a cart from a supermarket with all their earthly goods in the basket. I've seen poor people in Grand Central Station in New York City going from one refuse container to another looking for scraps of food that people have thrown away, so that they may eat. So it was with this beggar, Lazarus—he stood at the gate hoping to sustain himself, literally, from the garbage of the wealthy man.

Then we are told that the beggar died and was carried by the angels to "Abraham's bosom." We have to be careful here. Is Jesus teaching that any time a saint dies and goes to heaven that he is borne into the presence of God by these angelic messengers? Or is this imagery describing the great beauty of the afterlife? I don't know the answers to those question, but it's fun to speculate. It certainly doesn't violate any principle of Scripture to think that at the moment we die, we meet an escort, and that the escort or escorts are the angels who carry us into the presence of Christ. Wouldn't it be remarkable if, the moment we cease this life, we are immediately in the presence of the angels? There is at least one biblical precedent in our Lord's ascent into heaven in the presence of the angels who were there on the Mount of Ascension (Acts 1:9-11). So I like to think that this is normative, that Jesus is adding a detail here that is borrowed from the full content of biblical revelation, and that we, as His people, can look forward to an escort service that transcends any liveried limousine we ever might enjoy in this world.

Jesus calls the place to which the beggar is taken by the angels "Abraham's bosom." That term is sometimes used in our day as a nickname for heaven itself, the place where the father of the faithful is now resting in his eternal felicity. Then we're told that the rich man also died, but he went to Hades. There he could see Abraham and Lazarus "afar off." This does not necessarily mean that people who are in hell have the ability to see people who are in heaven, and vice versa, although, because Jesus draws this picture, it's hard to resist the inference that that is the case. At least for the purposes of His parable, Jesus tells the story such that the rich man, in the midst of his awful, dreadful torment, is able to see the splendor and joy that he is missing, and that the poor man is enjoying.

Jesus goes on to say, "Then he cried and said, 'Father Abraham, have mercy on me, and send Lazarus that he may dip the tip of his finger in water and cool my tongue, for I am tormented in this flame'" (v. 24). What can we draw from this? These words don't necessarily mean that hell is a place of fire, as we've already indicated, and that the torment is one of intense heat. The point Jesus is making is that the sinner in hell would give everything he had, do anything that he could do, to make the number of sins he committed in this world one less. The rich man is seeking some relief from his pain, and now he's begging for help from the beggar he ignored. He's not asking for a sumptuous dinner to be sent down from heaven. All he asks is that Lazarus would dip the tip of his finger in cool water and touch his tongue. "Give me the slightest bit of relief," is the cry of the rich man. It's also interesting that he makes this cry with these words: "Have mercy on me."

I wonder whether the rich man now understands that the torment he is suffering is just and that if any balm were to be given him for his pain, it would be, indeed, an act of mercy.

Next we read:

> But Abraham said, "Son, remember that in your lifetime you received your good things and likewise Lazarus evil things; but now he is comforted and you are tormented. And besides all this, between us and you there is a great gulf fixed, so that those who want to pass from here to you cannot, nor can those from there pass to us." Then he said, "I beg you therefore, father, that you would send him to my father's house, for I have five brothers, that he may testify to them, lest they also come to this place of torment." Abraham said to him, "They have Moses and the prophets; let them hear them." And he said, "No, father Abraham, but if one goes to them from the dead, they will repent." But he said to him, "If they do not hear Moses and the prophets, neither will they be persuaded though one rise from the dead." (vv. 25-31)

With this plea, the rich man begs that Abraham would send someone to talk to his brothers, lest they fall into the same misery he is experiencing. He wants someone to go and warn them of what waits for the impenitent beyond the grave. If Abraham won't rescue him, surely he will rescue the rich man's brothers who are still alive. The rich man seems to think that extraordinary measures are called for—that his brothers will believe only if something miraculous happens. But Abraham says that God's teaching through Moses and the prophets is sufficient. Those who do not believe God's revelation will not believe His miracles.

I think the principle point of this parable is this: There is a great gulf fixed between heaven and hell, and once a person goes to one or the other, there is no bridge from hell to heaven after death. As the Bible says, "it is appointed for men to die once, but after this the judgment" (Heb. 9:27). There is no second chance beyond the grave. And Jesus tells us, through the lips of Abraham, that how we die is final for all of us.

Perhaps one of the greatest follies we find ourselves committing is the folly of procrastination. We keep saying to ourselves that tomorrow we're going to turn over a new leaf. Tomorrow we will make ourselves right with God, but we're not quite ready. That was the thinking of the rich fool, and his foolishness was shown in the warning, "Fool! This night your soul will be required of you" (Luke 12:20a). We are not to postpone our redemption by such procrastination: "Behold, now is the accepted time; behold, now is the day of salvation" (2 Cor. 6:2b). Christ has come back from the grave. We have the opportunity now, today, to hear Him, flee to Him, and embrace Him. Today may be the last opportunity we will ever have.

PART THREE

———

Angels

9

The Heavenly Choir

In the second half of the twentieth century, one of the leading New Testament scholars in the world was Rudolf Bultmann, who was known for his critical analysis of the Scriptures. In a little book entitled *Kerygma and Myth*, he called on the church to "de-mythologize" the content of the Bible. He said that the Bible contains a mixture of history and what he called "mythology," that there is a kernel of historical truth encrusted within a husk of primitive mythology. Therefore, if modern humanity is to glean anything of value from the pages of Scripture, one must cut through that husk of mythology and reach the core, the kernel, of historical truth.

In one of his key statements in the book, Bultmann said that no one could live in the twentieth century and take advantage of modern science, use electricity, consume modern antibiotics, listen to radios, watch televisions, or turn on incandescent lights and still think of a universe that is constructed in three tiers, with the heavens above, hell beneath, and earth in the middle, populated by angels and demons. So when Bultmann leveled his critique against the so-called mythological content of the Bible, one dimension of that was the appearance and activity of angelic beings.

Many years ago, in the mining district of western Pennsylvania, not far from where I grew up, there was a terrible mine disaster. Men were trapped beneath the surface for a couple of weeks underground, and some weak tapping was heard. People waited for days and days with anxious anticipation and waning hopes that anyone would be rescued. Finally, two men who had been trapped underground were brought to the surface in fine condition. The morning edition of the *Pittsburgh Post Gazette* had a bold headline on the day of their rescue: "Miners Rescued by Miracle." The secular press did not hesitate to call the survival of these men, after all that time under the earth without food and water, a miracle. But the article had a sub-headline that said the men were suffering hallucinations. These men, when they were brought to the surface and were interviewed by the media, explained that they had been able to survive underground for so long because they were ministered to by an angel. They both attested to this experience. One of the men afterward became a minister and spent the rest of his life going around the United States, telling people the story of his rescue and of being ministered to by an angel. In any case, I found the dichotomy in the paper very strange. On the one hand, the paper attributed the men's rescue to supernatural intervention. On the other hand, the men's claim that they had been visited by an angel was dismissed as a hallucination.

The reason for that is easily explained. As Bultmann noted, the existence of angels is not a part of the modern worldview. They're not a part of our secular perception of reality. The modern mindset is to dismiss the presence of angels as at best merely incidental elements of the biblical witness, and we think that what's really important from the biblical witness is the teaching about sin and the love of God. But when we come to the text of Scripture, which is bathed in the supernatural and is awash with a flood of miracles, particularly concentrated during the ministry and life of Jesus Himself, we find angels.

When I was in college, my professor gave me the assignment of writing a paper on the subject of angels. I don't remember learning a great deal from that assignment, but one of the things I do recall is that I looked up the references to angels in the *Theological Dictionary of the New Testament*, and I discovered that the word *angelos*, which is the Greek word that is translated as "angel," occurs more frequently in the New Testament than the word we translate as "sin." The word *angelos* also occurs more frequently in the New Testament than the word *agape*, which is the chief and primary word for "love." When I made these discoveries, I knew I couldn't just push this subject to the edge of significance. Angels are part and parcel of the biblical message from early in creation, from the book of Genesis all the way to the book of Revelation. We don't simply see a flurry of angelic activity concentrated in the pages of the New Testament during the life of Jesus; we encounter them throughout the whole scope of redemptive history.

The word *angelos*, in its most basic definition, simply means "messenger," and there are times when *angelos* refers to a human messenger. Anyone who bears news can be called an "angel," and so we must make some kind of distinction between the heavenly beings that we call angels and earthly people who are engaged in the activity of message-bringing. But almost exclusively when the Scriptures use the term *angelos*, it is in reference to a supernatural or heavenly being, not just to an earthly messenger.

When we examine the references to angels in the Old and New Testaments, we can place the activity of angels into two distinct locations. There are different functions of angels in these locations, but first of all we must make a distinction between the locales in which we find them. The first is the heavenly realm. Much of what the Bible says about angels does not refer to their activity on earth but to their activity in heaven, and I want to look at some of the well-known texts wherein the heavenly mission of the angels is described.

Let me begin with one of my favorite texts, the sixth chapter of the book of Isaiah, where we have the record of Isaiah's vision into the heavenly temple. Isaiah tells us, "In the year that King Uzziah died, I saw the Lord sitting on a throne, high and lifted up, and the train of His robe filled His temple" (v. 1). After he gives this brief description of the elevated Lord in His splendor of exaltation, he goes on to say, "Above it stood seraphim; each one had six wings: with two he covered his face, with two he covered his feet, with two he flew.

And one cried to another and said, 'Holy, holy, holy is the LORD of hosts; the whole earth is full of His glory'" (vv. 2-3).

I have taught often on the holiness of God and written a book on the subject, and this is one of the most important texts on that topic, because here we have the first appearance in the Scriptures of the so-called *trisagion*, the three-times "holy," where that attribute of God is repeated in antiphonal response in the immediate presence of God by angelic beings. What the angels are doing here is worshiping God. They are, as it were, the heavenly choir, celebrating the transcendent majesty of the Creator by singing of His splendor and saying, "Holy, holy, holy."

Repetition is a Hebrew method for bringing emphasis. It is rare to find triple repetition in the Scriptures, but there are a number of instances of double repetition. When our Lord was teaching and wanted to indicate that something was especially important, He would say to His disciples, "Verily, verily, I say unto you," or, "Truly, truly, I say to you." That repetition was a tool for emphasis that the Jews used occasionally. But only in rare instances was something emphasized to the superlative degree by being mentioned three times. We find it in Jeremiah's temple speech, when he said that the hypocrisy of the people had reached superlative levels and commanded them, "Do not trust in these lying words, saying, 'The temple of the LORD, the temple of the LORD, the temple of the LORD are these'" (Jer. 7:4). We find it negatively in the book of Revelation, when the sounding of the last three trumpets is preceded by an angel warning, "Woe, woe, woe to the inhabitants of the earth, because of the

remaining blasts of the trumpet of the three angels"
(Rev. 8:13b), indicating the worst of all possible mani-
festations of misery. And here in Isaiah 6 we see the
holiness of God exalted to the third degree, and it's
done by angels, whose function is to minister in the
presence of God.

I'm interested in the physical description of the seraphim here in Isaiah. They are said to have six wings.
Two of the wings are used for flight. You would think
that the other four would be useless appendages, but
we know that God makes His creatures suitable for
their environments. When He creates fish, He gives
them gills, scales, and fins because their environment
is the water. When He makes birds, He gives them
lightweight skeletal structures, feathers, and wings
so that they can move through the air. So, when God
makes angels for His immediate presence, He gives
them six wings: two with which to fly, plus two to
cover their faces and two to cover their feet. Even the
angels, these heavenly creatures, when they are in the
immediate presence of the transcendent holiness of
God, must shield their eyes from His glory because it
is so dazzling. We are told in Scripture that God's glory is blinding to the eyes of creatures, even as Paul was
blinded by the light that he saw on the road to Damas-
cus. We saw earlier that when the book of Revelation
describes the New Jerusalem, it says there is no sun or
moon there, and yet there's no darkness, because the
city is illumined by the glory of God and of the Lamb.
It is in that immediate, intense brilliance of the divine
glory that the angels are called to minister with their
songs of praise and adoration. They are equipped by

God to shield their eyes from the heavenly vision that they enjoy every day.

Let me say in passing that we sometimes overlook that the New Testament teaches us that the worship of the saints in this world involves a mystical transcendence. The communion of saints means that we're no longer separated from the presence of God, as the people of Israel were, when they were called to come near Mount Sinai when God came down to visit and give His law. God initially allowed Moses to come up on the mountain, but all the rest of the people were forbidden from even touching the mountain, lest they be summarily executed (Exod. 19). But the author of Hebrews tells us we're no longer in that situation. We don't come now to a mountain that can't be touched by hands; now we ascend into the heavenly sanctuary, into the heavenly Jerusalem, so that when we come together for worship, mystically we participate in the immediate presence of God, in the presence of Christ, with the general assembly of the saints, of the spirits of just men made perfect, and of the angels (Heb. 12:18-24). So we're part of this choir when we gather for worship on Sunday morning. But this is the task that keeps the seraphim busy day after day after day—praising God in His sanctuary.

We also see that in addition to the two wings that cover their faces, the seraphim have two wings with which they cover their feet. That's not explained specifically in the text here, but I think that we can make legitimate inferences from the rest of Scripture as to why God equips the seraphim with a special set of wings to cover their feet. Remember the incident wherein Moses approaches the burning bush in the

Midianite wilderness, having seen the bush burning but not being consumed? He turns aside to look at it, and the voice speaks to him out of the bush saying, "Take your sandals off your feet, for the place where you stand is holy ground" (Exod. 3:5). What made the ground holy? It wasn't Moses that made it holy. It was that this piece of real estate was the place where God had descended to communicate in this special event with Moses. Because the presence of God has sanctified this spot, He tells Moses to take off his shoes. Why is that necessary? If you look through Scripture, you learn that we are of the dust and that we have feet of clay. It is our feet that attach us, as it were, to the creation, to the sphere in which we live out our days, of the earth. We're of the earth.

Well, angels are in heaven. Nevertheless, they are still creatures, and the sign of their creatureliness, just like the sign of our creatureliness, is their feet. So when they come into the presence of God, even though they're specially created for that purpose, not only do they cover their eyes from the glory of God, they cover their creatureliness from the divine view as they soar above the throne, singing constantly, "Holy, holy, holy is the LORD of hosts; the whole earth is full of His glory!"

10

The Heavenly Host

The *New King James Version* of the Bible includes subtitles throughout the text of Scripture. These subtitles are not part of the original text, of course; nevertheless, they are frequently helpful in giving the reader a sense of what a section of the biblical text is about. At the opening of Revelation 4, we find this subtitle: "The Throne Room of Heaven." In the previous chapter, we looked at Isaiah's vision of the heavenly throne room, and here we find that subject revisited in John's vision. Just as there were angels in Isaiah's vision, so there are angels in John's vision, and so we can learn more about these beings in this passage.

Revelation 4 reads:

> After these things I looked, and behold, a door standing open in heaven. And the first voice which I heard was like a trumpet speaking with me, saying, "Come up here, and I will show you things which must take place after this." Immediately I was in the Spirit; and behold, a throne set in

heaven, and One sat on the throne. And He who sat there was like a jasper and a sardius stone in appearance; and there was a rainbow around the throne, in appearance like an emerald. Around the throne were twenty-four thrones, and on the thrones I saw twenty-four elders sitting, clothed in white robes; and they had crowns of gold on their heads. And from the throne proceeded lightnings, thunderings, and voices. Seven lamps of fire were burning before the throne, which are the seven Spirits of God.

Before the throne there was a sea of glass, like crystal. And in the midst of the throne, and around the throne, were four living creatures full of eyes in front and in back. The first living creature was like a lion, the second living creature like a calf, the third living creature had a face like a man, and the fourth living creature was like a flying eagle. The four living creatures, each having six wings, were full of eyes around and within. And they do not rest day or night, saying, "Holy, holy, holy, Lord God Almighty, who was and is and is to come!" Whenever the living creatures give glory and honor and thanks to Him who sits on the throne, who lives forever and ever, the twenty-four elders fall down before Him who sits on the throne and worship Him who lives forever and ever, and cast their crowns before the throne, saying: "You are worthy, O Lord, to receive glory and honor and power; for You created all things, and by Your will they exist and were created." (vv. 1-11)

This passage is packed with vivid imagery. Much of the imagery is included in the famous hymn "Holy, Holy, Holy" by Reginald Heber. In that hymn we sing:

Holy, holy, holy! All the saints adore thee,
Casting down their golden crowns around the glassy sea;
Cherubim and seraphim falling down before thee
Who wert, and art, and evermore shall be.

Here again, then, we are privileged to look into the interior chamber of heaven, where we see angels. As

John's vision continues in Revelation 5, he tells us that the number of angels he saw in this throne room was "ten thousand times ten thousand" (5:11), or, as some versions render it, "myriads of myriads." These vast ranks of angels compose what we call the "heavenly host" (Luke 2:13). The word *host* does not refer to someone who is the master of ceremonies at a banquet or to a person who welcomes you to his home; here the term *host* is used as a synonym for *army*. This is why the Old Testament frequently refers to God as "the LORD of hosts" (1 Sam. 17:45; Ps. 46:7; Isa. 8:13). There is an army of angels who are sometimes called "seraphim," sometimes called "cherubim," terms that Scripture seems to use interchangeably.

Again we see here that the locale of the seraphim and the cherubim is in the immediate presence of God, where they praise and honor Him because He is worthy, and they shout that truth out day and night. Also, we're given more physical description here than in Isaiah 6. John describes four creatures that look like a calf, like a man, like a lion, and like an eagle, and they have eyes all over their bodies as they behold the presence of God. These angels are enjoying that which is the highest hope of the Christian—the beatific vision—and they are given many eyes with which to enjoy it. The beatific vision is so-called because it is the vision that results in the highest level of blessedness that any human creature can enjoy. This is the hope Jesus held out to one particular group in the Sermon on the Mount when He said, "Blessed are the pure in heart, for they shall see God" (Matt. 5:8). The promise of the vision of God is given to those who are pure, and so we are told that we must become holy, for without holiness no one will see God (Heb. 12:14).

Elsewhere, John talks about the astonishing love that God gives to us: "Behold what manner of love the Father has bestowed on us, that we should be called children of God! ... Beloved, now we are children of God; and it has not yet been revealed what we shall be, but we know that when He is revealed, we shall be like Him, for we shall see Him as He is" (1 John 3:1-2).

That's our greatest hope: We're going to have the vision of God; we are going to see Him.

We may wonder how, even in our resurrected bodies, we will be able to see God, who is by nature a spirit, and who is invisible. Jonathan Edwards gives a good answer to that question. In the first place, the big problem that hides the glory of God from our eyes is not a defect in our optic nerve. The defect is in the heart. Sin is the barrier between us and God, and as long as there is sin in our hearts, as long as we're not pure in heart, we're not going to see Him. That's why, after the fall, God made the universal prohibition, "No man shall see Me, and live" (Exod. 33:20b). Before sin entered into humanity, there was apprehension of His glory; there was the beatific vision. But Edwards speculates that the beatific vision will be even better than that which our first parents enjoyed, because it will be immediate.

I remember a brief conversation I once had with another fellow about a football game. I asked him if he had seen the game, and he said he had. I asked, "You mean you were there at the stadium?" He said, "No, I saw it on television." I said: "Well, then, you didn't see the game. You saw an electronic image or reproduction of the game—the game was mediated to you through the medium of television. You didn't see it live and in person." But when we go to a football game, even then, if we're actually in the stadium, we see light bouncing off physical objects and creating certain responses in our eyes and in the optic nerves. Even then, what we perceive in the external world is mediated to our minds through our physical senses. But Edwards says that when we see God in glory, we won't need eyes. We won't need optic nerves. The mind will have an immediate perception of the glory of God. That thought absolutely blows me away.

How amazing is the imagery of Scripture, the picture of these angels who enjoy the beatific vision with eyes all over their bodies, looking every possible way. There's no direction they can turn that will cause them to lose sight of the glory of God. It's a bit like a pack of turkeys. I can remember many times sitting in a tree stand when I was hunting turkeys, and I would be watching a group of turkeys making their way through the woods. My heart would start beating, and I would get more and more excited, hoping they wouldn't see me. They can see you bat your eye at a hundred yards. Not only that, they move in a particular way in a pack through the woods that seemingly enables them to see in every direction at once. At all times, there's a turkey looking to the back. Another one's looking to the right; another one's looking to the left; and another one's looking forward. Sitting in the tree stand, I could only hope that none of them would be looking up. By this arrangement, they have a panoramic view of their whole environment, so that if one of them sounds the alert, they all scram in an instant. That's why they're so hard to kill. They rely on teamwork, because no turkey can see behind itself. They need others looking back there. But the angels that are described here, the seraphim, have eyes all over, so that God never disappears from their line of sight as they enjoy the beatific vision moment after moment after moment.

Let me now turn your attention to the first chapter of the book of Ezekiel, which is one of the most difficult chapters to digest in terms of the richness of its imagery and symbolism. The book of Ezekiel begins with these words: "Now it came to pass in the thirtieth year, in the fourth month, on the fifth day of the month, as I was among the captives by the River Chebar, that the heavens were opened and I saw visions of God" (v. 1). Just as Isaiah and John were given the privilege of peering into the inner court of heaven, so Ezekiel also is given this heavenly view. He goes on to say:

> On the fifth day of the month, which was the fifth year of King Jehoiachin's captivity, the word of the LORD came expressly to Ezekiel the priest, the son of Buzi, in the land of the Chaldeans by the River Chebar, and the hand of the LORD was upon him there. Then I looked, and behold, a whirlwind was coming out of the north, a great cloud with raging fire engulfing itself; and brightness was all around it and radiating out if its midst like the color of amber, out of the midst of the fire. Also from within it came the likeness of four living creatures. And this was their appearance: they had the likeness of a man. Each one had four faces, and each one had four wings. Their legs were straight, and the soles of their feet were like the soles of calves' feet. They sparkled like the color of burnished bronze. The hands of a man were under their wings on their four sides; and each of the four had faces and wings. Their wings touched one another. The creatures did not turn when they went, but each one went straight forward. (vv. 2-9)

I've seen some bizarre attempts to paint this scene in a way that people can capture it, but I'm not sure they succeeded. What is Ezekiel seeing? He sees several creatures with wings, but notice first of all the elements in which these creatures appear—a whirlwind, a great cloud, a raging fire, brightness, and radiation out of the midst of the fire. What we see here is a theophany. *Theos* means "God" and *phaneros* is "a manifestation." So a theophany is a visible manifestation of the invisible God. In the Scriptures, the primary theophany for God is fire or some form of fire, such as the burning bush or the pillar of fire. We also see this image in the *shekinah* glory, the bright, radiant light that accompanies the presence of God.

Ezekiel sees all of these signs of deity, of the presence of God. And just as God is accompanied by angels in the visions of His heavenly throne room, so He is attended by the angels as His presence comes to Ezekiel. Much like what John beheld in his vision, Ezekiel sees four living creatures, and one particular feature about them that he records is that their wings touched one another. Where else do we find a description of angelic wings touching each other? When King Solomon built the temple in Jerusalem, he fashioned two cherubim of olive wood overlaid with gold (1 Kings 6:23-28). They stood on either side of the ark of the covenant. The ark contained the law of Moses, the terms of their contract with God, as well as some manna and the rod of Aaron. The ark was the throne of God that was placed in the Holy of Holies, and the cover was the mercy seat, where the offerings were made on the Day of Atonement, the one day in the year when the high priest would go into the Holy of Holies and bring about "reconciliation" by pouring blood on the cover of the throne of God. The wings of these golden angels touched. The ark was an earthly replica of the heavenly throne of God, which is always attended by an army of angels, the cherubim and the seraphim.

Thus, the heavenly host is not just a small choir of angels. It is an army of specially created, spiritual beings whose task it is to honor and worship God and to attend His throne.

11

Earthly Enforcers

As we have seen, Scripture is clear that angels minister to God around His throne. Thus, heaven is one of the two places in which we see angels ministering in the accounts we have in Scripture. But angels also minister in the physical realm. In this chapter, I want to turn our attention to the way in which angels function with respect to this world and to the created order.

The book of Job tells us that angels were present at the time of the creation of the universe as we know it. In chapter 38, after Job has, in some sense of defiance, demanded answers of God about his circumstances, God poses a series of questions for Job by way of rebuke. So the chapter opens with these words of God:

> "Who is this who darkens counsel by words without knowledge? Now prepare yourself like a man; I will question you, and you shall answer Me. Where were you when I laid the foundations of the earth? Tell Me, if you have understanding. Who determined its measurements?

Surely you know! Or who stretched the line upon it? To what were its foundations fastened? Or who laid its cornerstone, when the morning stars sang together, and all the sons of God shouted for joy?" (vv. 2-7)

Note the allusion in this poetic discourse to the morning stars singing together with the sons of God. Traditionally, interpreters of the book of Job see the reference to the sons of God who were present during the time of creation as a reference to angels. That interpretation has provoked a lot of speculation and controversy. In the early chapters of Genesis, after Cain kills his brother Abel, we read the list of the descendants of Seth and then the descendants of Cain, and we see a radical expansion of evil; and then we read that the daughters of men intermarried with the sons of God and produced a race of very deviant people (Gen. 6:2). Many commentators have taken that text to mean an intermarriage between human women and angelic beings, because the angels are referred to as "the sons of God" elsewhere. Personally, I believe that what was involved there was intermarriage between the descendants of Cain and the descendants of Seth; this intermarriage created the final corruption of the whole race. But we do see the term "sons of God" used in the Bible to refer to angels.

If we look again at Job 38:7, we read, "When the morning stars sang together, and all the sons of God shouted for joy." This is an interesting poetic image, because it involves the personification of stars, attributing to the stars in the sky personal characteristics, such as singing. This suggests that at the earliest stages of creation, when God set the stars in the sky, the stars celebrated creation along with the sons of God, who shouted for joy. So we know that the angels were present at some time during creation, and we know that the angels themselves are created beings. That's important, and it will become even more important later on when we look at fallen angels, and especially at the biblical concept of Satan, because in our day the tendency is to attribute to Satan divine attributes, and to forget that Satan is a creature. Even though the angels that we've been examining so far are attending the immediate presence of God and therefore are heavenly beings, they are still creatures who were there during the creation of this natural world.

Now we know that after creation, God sustains everything that He made in this world and that He rules over the created sphere. The laws of nature are His laws, and the outworking of history follows the pattern of His sovereign rule. We do not believe God created everything and then, like the god of deism, stepped out of the picture: that He wound up the clock and now is simply letting it run down according to its own internal, mechanical operation. Rather, we believe that the God who created the universe also sustains that universe. He keeps it in existence and rules over it. One of the ways in which God mediates His providential supervision and rule over history and over creation is through the mission of these creatures that He formed to carry out His will, namely, the angels.

The first appearance of angels in the Bible happens early in the book of Genesis (apart from the appearance of Satan, the fallen angel whom we'll treat separately). We see a strange phenomenon after Adam and Eve fall and are expelled from the Garden of Eden. They are

forced to live east of Eden, and they are not permitted
to seek sanctuary or residence back in the garden. They
may have had a strong desire to regain the enjoyment
of the Edenic paradise, but they were not able to come
back into the garden. Why not? Because God posted
sentries at the entrance to the Garden of Eden, and
the sentries who were carrying out God's providential
government at that point in history were angels with
a flaming sword (Gen. 3:24).

Although this is just a brief mention of the function
of certain angels in the early chapters of Genesis, it's
pregnant with significance for our understanding of
the doctrine of providence. First of all, we need to see
that this incident, when God posted the angels at the
entrance to the Garden of Eden, is the first representation of government in Scripture, at least in terms of
law enforcement. The first law enforcement officers in
human history were not even human beings, but angels who bore the sword against potential evildoers.

This glimpse of angelic activity, along with other
passages that we'll look at in this chapter, has provoked
some fascinating studies about the role of angels in human government. One of the most respected biblical
scholars of the twentieth century was a Swiss by the
name of Oscar Cullman, and while many theologians
spend little time studying the role and the function
of angels in redemptive history, Cullman broke that
mold and did extensive studies of angels and wrote
essays concerning the concept of angelic powers in
Scripture. His idea was that there is a providential rule
of each government in the world by angelic powers,
some of which are good and some of which are evil.
The Scriptures tell us that God raises up kingdoms

and tears down kingdoms, but Cullman was getting at the way in which He raises them up or tears them down; he said God does it through the mediation of angelic beings. When Paul tells us to put on the whole armor of God in the New Testament, he tells us that we need to do so because our struggle in this world is not with flesh and blood, but against "principalities, against powers, against the rulers of the darkness of this age, against spiritual hosts of wickedness in the heavenly places" (Eph. 6:12). That is, in the heavenly spheres there are evil powers that have evil influence mediated through powers and principalities, which are earthly governments. So Paul is saying that the people of God need to have the whole armor of God, because their struggle is not just against people but against governments that have been or can be demonized; that standing behind these worldly forces and authorities are supernatural powers that for the most part remain invisible to us.

But we do not have only these demonic powers involved in world governments, such that governments can become empires of evil. There are also agents of God for good who are involved in nations and in governments. We find an example of that in the book of Daniel, where we read: "At that time Michael shall stand up, the great prince who stands watch over the sons of your people, and there shall be a time of trouble, such as never was since there was a nation, even to that time. And at that time your people shall be delivered ..." (12:1a).

Michael is identified earlier in the book of Daniel as an archangel. We distinguish levels of authority among the angelic hosts in Scripture, and the difference between an archangel and an angel is simply a difference in rank and authority. The word *arche* in Greek means "in the beginning," "chief," or "ruler." John uses it in the first verse of his Gospel when he writes, "In the beginning was the Word ...." Usually, however, the word is used to refer to that which is in the highest place of authority. It comes across into English as the prefix "arch." We have enemies and we have archenemies. In football, we have rivals and we have archrivals. The Roman Catholic Church has bishops and archbishops. In construction, we have builders and we have architects, which literally means "chief builders." So we see this word frequently used in the English language.

Well, it also functions that way in the Greek, and we can distinguish between an angel and an archangel. The angels who are archangels are commanders of the heavenly host, who are seated in positions of authority to exercise God's rule and authority over creation. And one of those who is named in Scripture is Michael, who appears here in the book of Daniel as the angelic manifestation of the power of God to redeem His nation. Also, Gabriel is understood in biblical history to be an archangel, and we will look at his activity later on, as he serves as the chief messenger of God in Scripture.

The angels that we encounter in the Old Testament often manifest themselves in human form. Let's take an example that we find in Genesis 18. The passage says, "Then the LORD appeared to him [Abraham] by the terebinth trees of Mamre, as he was sitting in the tent door in the heat of the day. So he lifted his eyes and looked, and behold, three men were standing by him; and when he saw them, he ran from the tent door to meet them, and bowed himself to the ground, and said, 'My Lord, if I have now found favor in Your sight, do not pass on by Your servant'" (vv. 1-3).

There is something a little difficult here. Angels are not to be worshiped, and yet the response of Abraham to these three who come to him by the oaks of Mamre is a response of worship. He falls on his face before them, which causes many commentators to believe that what we have here are two regular angels plus the Angel of the Lord, who is so closely connected with God that he wears, as it were, the very mantle of God and can be seen as either a theophany or as a christophany, that is, an outward manifestation of God Himself or as an outward manifestation of the preincarnate Christ. Many people believe that Melchizedek (Gen. 14) was really Christ appearing in the Old Testament in human form, and the commander of the LORD's army in Joshua is also often seen as a christophany (Josh. 5).

In any case, we find these three, who appear here in Genesis to consult with Abraham, and Abraham says: "Please let a little water be brought, and wash your feet, and rest yourselves under the tree. And I will bring a morsel of bread, that you may refresh your hearts" (vv. 4-5a). They go on to have a conversation in which Abraham intercedes for the future of Sodom. Then, in chapter 19, we read:

Now the two angels [presumably the two angels without the Angel of the Lord] came to Sodom in the evening, and Lot was sitting in the gate of Sodom. When Lot saw them, he rose to meet them, and he bowed himself with his face toward the ground. And he said, "Here now, my lords, please turn in to your servant's house and spend the night, and wash your feet; then you may rise early and go on your way." And they said, "No, but we will spend the night in the open square." But he insisted strongly; so they turned in to him and entered his house. Then he made them a feast, and baked unleavened bread, and they ate. Now before they lay down, the men of the city, the men of Sodom, both old and young, all the people from every quarter, surrounded the house. And they called to Lot and said to him, "Where are the men who came to you tonight. Bring them out to us that we may know them carnally." (vv. 1-5)

Apparently, these angels are so magnificently attractive that the Sodomites seek to use them sexually. As the story progresses, Lot, trying to protect the angels, offers his daughters to the crowd instead. They'll have none of that, but what's significant for our concern is in verses 9-11: "And they said, 'Stand back!' Then they said, 'This one came in to stay here, and he keeps acting as a judge; now we will deal worse with you than with them.' So they pressed hard against the man Lot, and came near to break down the door. But the men reached out their hands and pulled Lot into the house with them, and shut the door. And they struck the men who were at the doorway of the house with blindness, both small and great, so that they became weary trying to find the door."

So these angels, who are supposed to receive biblical hospitality in the house of Lot, intercede to save Lot and his family, pulling him away from the mob, into the safety in the house, and then using their powers to strike the wicked Sodomites blind. In this case, the angels are there to minister to Lot and to his family in a time of crisis. That's a key that we want to hold onto for future consideration, because that also is one of the functions of the angels that God sends to work out His providential rule over history.

12

Angels as Ministers

One of my favorite angel narratives in all of Scripture is found in the second book of Kings, and I enjoy this particular narrative because it reveals, directly and indirectly, many important things about the nature and function of angels. It is a narrative that takes place during the life of the prophet Elisha. It begins this way: "Now the king of Syria was making war against Israel; and he consulted with his servants, saying, 'My camp will be in such and such a place.' And the man of God sent to the king of Israel, saying, 'Beware that you do not pass this place, for the Syrians are coming down there.' Then the king of Israel sent someone to the place of which the man of God had told him. Thus he warned him, and he was watchful there, not just once or twice" (6:8-10).

The king of Syria is trying to plan an ambush against the king of Israel. Somehow, all of the secret plans that the king of Syria is making are told to the king of Israel, so he avoids the trap. Then we read, "Therefore the heart of the king of Syria was greatly troubled by this thing; and he called his servants and said to them, 'Will you not show me which of us is for the king of Israel?'" (v. 11). He automatically assumes that he has a spy in the camp, so he inquires about it. "And one of his servants said, 'None, my lord, O king; but Elisha, the prophet who is in Israel, tells the king of Israel the words that you speak in your bedroom.' So he said, 'Go and see where he is, that I may send and get him.' And it was told him, saying, 'Surely he is in Dothan'" (vv. 12-13).

You get the picture. The king of Syria is told that it's not one of his men who are betraying him, but that his plans are being communicated supernaturally by the prophet Elisha to the king of Israel. So, the king of Syria changes his plan. He thinks, "If I'm ever going to capture the king of Israel, the first thing I must do is get rid of Elisha." He inquires as to where Elisha is staying, and he's told that Elisha is in Dothan. So he sets about to execute his plan to capture Elisha.

The narrative continues: "Therefore he sent horses and chariots and a great army there, and they came by night and surrounded the city. And when the servant of the man of God arose early and went out, there was an army, surrounding the city with the horses and chariots. And his servant said to him, 'Alas, my master! What shall we do?'" (vv. 14-15). Elisha goes to sleep in Dothan. His servant gets up first thing in the morning, goes outside, and sees all the chariots and soldiers of the Syrians. Then he goes to the other side of the house, but he still sees nothing but chariots. He goes to the front and he goes to the back, but there are chariots everywhere. So he runs and wakes Elisha, and he tells him of the predicament. He says: "We're surrounded by chariots and armies. What are we going to do?"

Listen to Elisha's response. "So he answered, 'Do not fear, for those who are with us are more than those who are with them'" (v. 16). I can only imagine that Elisha's servant is completely flabbergasted by Elisha's words. "You don't get it," he probably says. "I just told you there are countless soldiers and chariots around us, but here there's only you and me. What do you mean that those who are with us are more than those who are with them?"

Then we read: "And Elisha prayed, and said, 'LORD, I pray, open his eyes that he may see.' Then the LORD opened the eyes of the young man, and he saw. And behold, the mountain was full of horses and chariots of fire all around Elisha. So when the Syrians came down to him, Elisha prayed to the LORD, and said, 'Strike this people, I pray, with blindness.' And He struck them with blindness according to the word of Elisha" (vv. 17-18).

There are so many things that we can learn from this passage. One has to do with an ongoing controversy among theologians in the history of the church over the idea of guardian angels. In the New Testament, Jesus tells His disciples not to forbid little children to come to Him, "for of such is the kingdom of God" (Luke 18:16b). Elsewhere He says, "Take heed that you do not despise one of these little ones, for I say to you that in heaven their angels always see the face of My Father who is in heaven" (Matt. 18:10). The idea that was extrapolated from that statement of our Lord was that every person in the kingdom—every Christian—has a guardian angel assigned to take care of him or her. As we will see

a bit later, the author of Hebrews tells us that the primary function of angels, in terms of this world, is to minister to God's people. So there is a strong tradition in
church history that every person has a particular angel
assigned to him. But what we find in this story of Elisha
is that there is not just one angel watching out for him,
but the whole heavenly host is mobilized to defend him
in his critical hour of need.

In chapter 9, I related the story of a pair of miners
who were trapped underground for several days and
how they testified that they had been ministered to
by angels. That was how they explained their survival. The news media automatically assumed that they
were hallucinating, and the assumption in the secular world in which we live is that anyone who claims
to see an angel must be suffering hallucinations, for
a hallucination occurs, by definition, when someone
sees things that aren't really there. I also mentioned
how Rudolf Bultmann said we can't live in our sophisticated society and still believe in ghosts and goblins
and things that go bump in the night, or in invisible
realities such as angels.

But at the heart of the Judeo-Christian worldview
is an uncompromised supernaturalism that says that
there is much more to reality than meets the eye. God
Himself is invisible, and yet there's nothing more central to Christianity than the reality of the existence of
God. The thing that makes it so difficult for us to be
faithful to God, I believe, is that He's invisible, and it's
hard to worship that which you do not see and to obey
One you've never heard speak, and so on. But the same
thing may be true of angels. They're invisible most of
the time. There are times throughout biblical history,

as we read in the case of the visitors to Sodom and elsewhere, when the angels manifest themselves, usually in human garb, but under ordinary circumstances, they conceal themselves. They're real; they're creatures; but they're also spirit beings who are invisible. If we really do believe in the message of the Christian faith, we have to understand that the reality in which we live contains much more than meets the eye.

Now, that should not be too much of a stretch for us, living on this side of the Enlightenment, on this side of the invention of the telescope, on this side of the invention of the microscope, because the scientific revolution of the modern era has increased and enhanced our perception of reality by means of instruments that enable us to see things that cannot be seen with the naked eye. One of the crises in the time of Galileo was that the scientists of his day, as well as the bishop of his city, refused to put their eyes on his telescope because they didn't want to believe the evidence that the telescope was revealing about how the heavens really are structured and how the planets travel in their orbits. The Copernican revolution was a revolution in science that was provoked by a sudden ability to see what previously was unseen. If that revolution took place with the invention of the telescope, how much greater is the revolution that has taken place in our lifetimes with the microscope. There are millions of real entities in the air around each of us, and if we could see them with the naked eye, the sight would probably strike terror into our souls. But fortunately for us, we go along our merry ways, completely oblivious to the myriads of microbes that have the capacity to kill us.

So, we have learned through modern science that there are realities out there beyond the scope of our ability to perceive them. Why is it that we believe that germs that we can't see are out there, but we have a bias that says there cannot be supernatural, heavenly beings—spirit beings—like angels, even though the Scripture texts are full of them? That's one of the things that I love about this story: the servant couldn't see what was really there until Elisha prayed and said, "Please, Lord, open his eyes, let him see what's really out there." When God opened his eyes, the servant saw that the assembled host of angels was vastly superior in number and power to all of the chariots and armies of the king of Syria.

A similar incident is recorded in the New Testament during the account of the temptation of Jesus. Immediately after Jesus' baptism, the Spirit leads Him into the Judean wilderness to be tempted of Satan. The Devil suggests that Jesus isn't really the Son of God, even though the last words that Jesus had heard before going into the wilderness were those of the Father speaking from heaven: "This is My beloved Son, in whom I am well pleased" (Matt. 3:17). Satan says, "If You are the Son of God, command that these stones become bread" (4:3). That is the first temptation, to which Jesus responds by saying, "It is written, 'Man shall not live by bread alone, but by every word that proceeds from the mouth of God'" (v. 4). He was saying: "I am involved in a fast here. I'm involved in a test. I'm sorry, Satan, but I'm not going to turn those stones into bread. I can do it, but I don't have the permission of My Father to do it; so get away from Me." Then He quotes Scripture to Satan.

In the midst of this temptation, Satan quotes Scripture back to Jesus. When he takes Jesus to the pinnacle of the temple and urges Him to throw Himself down, he says, "It is written: 'He shall give His angels charge over you,' and, 'In their hands they shall bear you up, lest you dash your foot against a stone'" (v. 6b). Jesus had to correct the Devil's hermeneutic and say, "It is written again, 'You shall not tempt the LORD your God'" (v. 7). He's saying: "Yes, the Bible says that, but you have to interpret Scripture by Scripture. You can't set Scripture against Scripture, and the Bible also says, 'You shall not tempt the Lord your God.' So I'm not going to do what you suggest."

When the temptations are finished and Satan has departed, we are told, almost as a footnote, that angels come and minister to Jesus (v. 11). They were there all the time. It makes you wonder whether He could see them, as Elisha could. But God had given His angels charge over Him, and the angels came to Him in the midst of that crisis in His life. Immediately after the fallen angel departs, the heavenly host comes, and they minister to Jesus.

It's significant that this host of angels attends Jesus again and again throughout His lifetime, not only at the announcement of His birth, which we will look at separately, but also at the time of His resurrection. When the disciples come to the tomb, angels are there, in the garden or in the tomb itself, according to the various accounts. They say to the women who come to anoint Jesus' body: "Why do you seek the living among the dead? He is not here, but is risen!" (Luke 24:5b-6a). These angels are the escorts of Christ when He ascends into heaven, when He goes to His enthronement for His coronation as the King of kings.

When I think of the events that transpired during the life of Jesus, I ask myself, "If I could have been an eyewitness of any event in the life of Jesus, which one would

I choose?" That's really a hard question for me. Obviously, I would have been delighted to witness the resurrection. Who wouldn't? That would have been fantastic. But it's hard for me to choose between the resurrection and the transfiguration. To have seen that bursting forth of the glory of Christ through the veil of His humanity, where His countenance was changed, would have been incredible.

But there is another event that I really savor, because I've been to the Holy Land. I remember the time we went to Bethlehem, and we went to the Church of the Nativity and took the guided tour, and I was not really engaged by that. I left the company of those who were taking the tour and walked out by myself to the edge of the church. There was a primitive stone wall, and I went out and sat on that stone wall. It looks out onto a vast plain, the fields of Bethlehem, and I just let my imagination run wild. I sat there and imagined that night, pitch dark, maybe a little campfire bursting through the darkness, peasants sitting around, trying to keep warm, trying to watch over their flocks. Suddenly, all heaven breaks loose with the glory of God shining around as the heavenly hosts begin to sing of the birth of Christ. Oh, if I had seen that, I would have said like Simeon, "Lord, now You are letting Your servant depart in peace" (Luke 2:29), for I would have seen all I ever needed to see.

The angels attend our Lord in the manifestation of His glory. But when the glory of God is eclipsed in a culture and in the church, as it is in our day, angels are dismissed as insignificant. When the glory of God is honored and the exaltation of Christ is upheld, we see attending those moments the heavenly host, who serve as an escort for the King.

13

Angels as Messengers

One of the major tasks of angels is to serve as messengers for God. This function is clearly demonstrated in the birth narratives of the Gospels, and perhaps preeminently in the first chapter of the Gospel of Luke. There we read:

> There was in the days of Herod, the king of Judea, a certain priest named Zacharias, of the division of Abijah. His wife was of the daughters of Aaron, and her name was Elizabeth. And they were both righteous before God, walking in all the commandments and ordinances of the Lord blameless. But they had no child, because Elizabeth was barren, and they were both well advanced in years. And so it was, that while he was serving as priest before God in the order of his division, according to the custom of the priesthood, his lot fell to burn incense when he went into the temple of the Lord. And the whole multitude of the people was praying outside at the hour of incense. Then an angel of the Lord appeared to him, standing on the right side of the altar of incense. And when Zacharias saw him, he was troubled, and fear fell upon him. (vv. 5-12)

Zacharias was a priest of the tribe of Levi. The Jews' central sanctuary was the temple in Jerusalem, and it was the practice that local priests from the various districts around the nation were selected by lottery to have one turn in their lifetime, if they were fortunate enough, to serve in the temple of Jerusalem. Zacharias won the lottery, the unforgettable experience of going up to Jerusalem to participate in the ministry of the temple—in this case, going in and offering prayer at the altar of incense in the Holy Place. On this occasion, when the priest would go in, he would pray for the nation, and so it would always attract a large group of people who would surround the temple and watch the priest go in and wait for him to come out. It was something like what happens during the election of a pope. Huge throngs of people gather around in St Peter's Square and watch the chimney of the Sistine Chapel to see the smoke that comes out. If it's black, that means the vote has failed to elect a new pope; if it's white, that signifies that a new pope has been elected, and the people go wild when they see that sign. In the same way, the people in Jerusalem awaited the return of the priest, because if he came forth quickly, that meant the prayers had been offered and God had favorably heard the intercession of the priest.

However, on the day Zacharias goes in to pray, there is a delay. The cause is a radically unexpected intervention in the life of Zacharias as he is ministering in the temple. There appears to him an angel, and Scripture records that "he was troubled, and fear fell upon him."

That's noteworthy for this reason: The biblical worldview is unintelligible apart from the biblical teaching of the reality of the angelic world. But in our culture and in our time, there is skepticism about these things, because people say the perception of angels is not part of our common experience. When we look back to the Bible, we sort of "telescope" the events in the Bible and assume that angels were appearing every fifteen minutes. That's not the case, though angels did appear from time to time. We forget how many events were occurring in addition to those recorded in Scripture. The visible manifestation of one of these spirit beings was actually extraordinarily rare. Normally the angels were invisible, as was the case with Elisha and his servant, so that Elisha had to pray that his servant's eyes would be opened in order for him to see the reality that was there. When we see that this priest is devastated by fear when the angel appears, that should alert us to the rarity of that kind of experience even then. Zacharias was not accustomed to meeting and speaking with angels every day.

Luke then writes:

> But the angel said to him, "Do not be afraid, Zacharias, for your prayer is heard; and your wife Elizabeth will bear you a son, and you shall call his name John. And you will have joy and gladness, and many will rejoice at his birth. For he will be great in the sight of the Lord, and shall drink neither wine nor strong drink. He will also be filled with the Holy Spirit, even from his mother's womb. And he will turn many of the children of Israel to the Lord their God. He will also go before Him in the spirit and power of Elijah, 'to turn the hearts of the fathers to the children,' and the disobedient to the wisdom of the just, to make ready a people prepared for the Lord." And Zacharias said to the angel, "How shall I know this? For I am an old man, and my wife is well advanced in years." And the angel an-

swered and said to him, "I am Gabriel, who stands in the presence of God, and was sent to speak to you and bring you these glad tidings. But behold, you will be mute and not able to speak until the day these things take place, because you did not believe my words which will be fulfilled in their own time." (vv. 13-20)

The angel identifies himself as Gabriel. Only two angels in all of Scripture are identified by name—Michael, whom we looked at already, and Gabriel. Both Michael and Gabriel are said to be emissaries sent from the immediate presence of God, and to hold the rank of archangel, a commander of the host of heaven. Notice that Gabriel's function in this setting is, first of all, to be a messenger. He delivers a message. He makes an announcement. He tells Zacharias what is going to come to pass. But not only does he bring a message, he speaks the command of God. So he's not a mere messenger boy sent to communicate some information; he comes from the presence of God with the authority of his divine Master upon him to command Zacharias to do certain things. One of the things that he commands is that this child that is to be born is to follow a certain order of behavior in his life, similar to the Nazirite experience.

Another command is that the child's name is to be John. This command is significant because, in the Jewish tradition, whoever names someone or something has authority over that thing or person. For instance, the first task that God gave to human beings in the Garden of Eden was to name the animals, showing the dominion of humans over the animal kingdom. The animals didn't name Adam; Adam named the animals. Historically, throughout biblical history, when children are born, it is the parents of the child who have the authority to name the child. But on rare circumstances, that authority is withheld from the parents, and God intervenes into the situation, indirectly saying, "This child will serve Me in a special way, and so I am reserving for Myself the right to give his name." So, the angel comes from the presence of God and says: "Look, you're not going to call your son Zacharias Jr., and you're not going to name him after Uncle Abraham. His name shall be John."

Zacharias is dazed by unbelief. He finds this message very hard to believe. So the angel says that he will be mute until the things announced by the angel take place. Months later, when the family comes together to name this child, they're considering different names, including naming the child after his father, Zacharias (Luke 1:59). But Elizabeth declares that his name is to be John. The family is shocked, so they ask Zacharias, and he writes on a tablet, "His name is John" (Luke 1:63). He submits to the authority of the mandate that was given to him by Gabriel, and when he manifests his obedience, his ability to speak is restored.

Gabriel is sent on another mission in the first chapter of Luke's Gospel. We read:

> Now in the sixth month the angel Gabriel was sent by God to a city of Galilee named Nazareth, to a virgin betrothed to a man whose name was Joseph, of the house of David. The virgin's name was Mary. And having come in, the angel said to her, "Rejoice, highly favored one, the Lord is with you; blessed are you among women." But when she saw him, she was troubled at his saying, and considered what manner of greeting this was. Then the angel said to her, "Do not be afraid, Mary, for you have found favor with God. And behold, you will conceive in your womb and bring forth a Son, and shall call His name

JESUS. He will be great, and will be called the Son of the Highest; and the Lord God will give Him the throne of His father David. And He will reign over the house of Jacob forever, and of His kingdom there will be no end." Then Mary said to the angel, "How can this be, since I do not know a man?" And the angel answered and said to her, "The Holy Spirit will come upon you, and the power of the Highest will overshadow you; therefore, also, that Holy One who is to be born will be called the Son of God. Now indeed, Elizabeth your relative has also conceived a son in her old age; and this is now the sixth month for her who was called barren. For with God nothing will be impossible." Then Mary said, "Behold the maidservant of the Lord! Let it be to me according to your word." And the angel departed from her. (vv. 26-38)

This passage is the source of a huge controversy in church history, a controversy that goes on even in our own day. In the Roman Catholic Church, there are two camps that are strongly divided theologically in terms of their understanding of the role of Mary in redemptive history. These camps are called the maximalists and the minimalists. The minimalists think that Mary has a significant role, but they want to minimize it; the maximalists think of Mary as Co-Redemptrix with Christ, and they hold to what they call the Eve/Mary parallel. In the New Testament, a parallel is drawn between the destructive impact of Adam and the redemptive impact of Christ as the new Adam. The Eve/Mary parallel goes along the same vein: just as through one woman the world is plunged into ruin because of her disobedience, by another woman's obedience—Mary's—redemption comes into the world. So, members of this camp want to maximize her position.

It is in the context of this discussion that we find references to what is called "Mary's Fiat." When Gabriel tells Mary that the Holy Spirit will overshadow her and she will bring forth a child who will be the Son of God, her response to Gabriel is this: "Let it be to me according to your word." She's saying, "So be it." The construction in which she responds to the angel is in the imperative, and that is where the word *fiat* appears; the Latin word *fiat* is translated as "let it be." So, the theory is that Christ could not have been born apart from this imperative of Mary. By contrast, the Protestant understanding of this text is that Mary's expression is one of emphatic acquiescence to the authority of God, whose message has come to her, and it's a sign not of her authority over Gabriel but of her willingness, in a servant's posture, to be obedient to the call that has been given to her by God.

So here we see, again, the angel functioning both as messenger and as authoritative communicator of the Word of God.

There is one last passage I want to call to your attention regarding the visitation of angels, but it is one that has been somewhat problematic and enigmatic. We find it in the fifth chapter of the book of Joshua, when Joshua is preparing his army to go against Jericho. The people of Israel have realized that Jericho is a fortress and that the soldiers of Jericho are formidable, so if Joshua and his troops are going to be victorious in the conquest of Canaan, they're going to have to get past Jericho. Just before the battle occurs, Joshua has a memorable experience: "And it came to pass, when Joshua was by Jericho, that he lifted his eyes and looked, and behold, a Man stood opposite him with His sword drawn in His hand. And Joshua went to Him and said to Him, 'Are You for us or for our adversaries?'" (Josh. 5:13).

Joshua has an eye for military talent. He can see that this man looks like a formidable warrior, but he has never seen him before, and he's not sure whether he's one of his own soldiers that he has never met or if this is a ringer brought in to fight for the inhabitants of Jericho. So Joshua wants to find out whose team he is on. He goes up to the stranger and says, "Are you for us or for our adversaries?" The answer is wonderful. The answer is, "No." He says, "No, but as Commander of the army of the LORD I have now come" (v. 14a). With that, Joshua falls on his face to the earth and worships him. And Joshua says, "'What does my Lord say to His servant?' Then the Commander of the LORD's army said to Joshua, 'Take your sandal off your foot, for the place where you stand is holy.' And Joshua did so" (vv. 14b-15).

We have seen that Gabriel and Michael have the title of archangel, or commander of the heavenly host. But as we will see in the next chapter, angels are never to be worshiped. Yet here we see Joshua falling down and worshiping the Commander of the army of the LORD, with no subsequent rebuke from the angel. When humans do worship angels, the angels always stop them; since this angel accepts worship from Joshua, most scholars believe that what we have here is a pre-incarnation christophany—that this Commander is Christ. When He appears to Joshua and Joshua says, "Are you for us or for them?", the Commander replies: "No, I'm taking over. It's not a question of whether I am for you, but whether you are for Me."

14

Angel Worship?

In antiquity, the issue of whether or not Christians should give worship or veneration to angelic beings became a major problem. Adherents to certain Eastern religions openly practiced the worship of angels. Because some of the converts to Christianity brought these habits with them from pagan culture, there emerged the problem of Christians involved in angel worship. The Christian community had to deal with this issue. Paul's letter to the Colossians, for example, is one of his epistles that deals specifically with the issue of angel worship; but nowhere do we find a more comprehensive view of the superiority of Christ over angels than in the book of Hebrews.

Again, angels are heavenly beings who come from the very presence of God, but even so, they are creatures, and to ascribe worship to a creature of even the highest importance or rank is to engage in the sin of idolatry. In Paul's letter to the Romans, in the very first chapter, he writes that the wrath of God is revealed from heaven against all unrighteousness and ungodliness of men, who suppress the truth and hold it in unrighteousness, and so on, and what he gets at there is our propensity toward idolatry—serving and worshiping the creature rather than the Creator. The first, second, third, and fourth commandments all prohibit, in one way or another, any involvement in the worship of a creature.

The book of Hebrews opens with these words: "God, who at various times and in various ways spoke in time past to the fathers by the prophets, has in these last days spoken to us by His Son, whom He has appointed heir of all things, through whom also He made the worlds" (vv. 1-2). This is not the only place in sacred Scripture where Christ is revealed as the Creator of the universe. In John's Gospel, the Word is identified as the One by whom and through whom all things were made. The book of Colossians also stresses what we call the "cosmic Christ," the Creator of the universe. So, the things that call attention to the uniqueness of Christ in this opening word show why He is the consummate revelation of God. God spoke in various ways in various times in the past, but now He has spoken in this way: by the One who is God's heir and who is the Creator. Christ alone is the appointed heir of the Father. We become joint-heirs with Him by virtue of our adoption, but only Christ has, as it were, the natural or essential relationship to the Father as the only begotten Son, as the rightful heir of God.

Then the author of Hebrews goes on with this marvelous verse: "Who being the brightness of His glory and the express image of His person, and upholding all things by the word of His power, when He had by Himself purged our sins, sat down at the right hand of the Majesty on high" (v. 3). This is as high a Christology as you will find anywhere in the Bible. When we think about the glory of God, the refulgent majesty that blazes from time to time through biblical history—such as in the Shekinah cloud, in the glory that surrounded the appearance of the angels around Bethlehem, in the glory cloud that takes Christ up to heaven, and so on—we think of a brilliant light that is associated with the glory of God. The author of Hebrews says that the Son is the very brightness of that glory; that is, He belongs to the essence of the divine being. Again, in the biblical period, to ascribe glory was to ascribe deity. Glory was principally a divine attribute. One of the most important early hymns of the Christian church was the "Gloria Patri," in which we sing as follows:

"Glory be to the Father and to the Son and to the Holy Ghost.
As it was in the beginning, is now and ever shall be
World without end, amen. Amen."

That is an eternal concept of divine glory that has no beginning in time and no end in time. It is something that goes forever. So here in Hebrews, the glory of Christ, as the brightness of the Father's glory, is affirmed as the express image of His person.

This may mean that Jesus manifests to us the perfection of the image of God like no other human being ever has. When Adam was disobedient to God, he failed to manifest and reflect the holiness of God, and that's every human being's sin. We're still the image of God in a certain sense, but that image has been tarnished so that we cannot accurately reflect the perfection of God's holiness, which is what we were created to do. Of course, the only one who ever achieved that perfect reflection or manifestation of divine holiness was Jesus. So we might read in this text that He is the express image of the Father's person, that He is the perfect image-bearer, referring to His humanity.

However, I think the author has something else in mind when he writes this, because he says that Jesus is the brightness of the divine glory. That's an affirmation of His deity. He's the express image of the divine person of the Father. That seems to be the import of what the author is saying in this text. However, this is all anticipatory for what comes next. He writes that Jesus is "upholding all things by the word of His power, [and] when He had by Himself purged our sins, sat down at the right hand of the Majesty on high, having become so much better than the angels, as He has by inheritance obtained a more excellent name than they" (vv. 3-4).

Now, the emphasis in this passage may be shifting to the ministry of the incarnate Christ, because obviously there is no elevation of the divine nature above the angels as a result of some kind of earthly ministry. The elevation above the angels is the elevation of the incarnate Christ over the angels. The psalmist asks, "When I consider Your heavens, the work of Your fingers, the moon and the stars, which You have ordained, what is man that You are mindful of him, and the son of man that You visit him? For you have made him a little lower than the angels" (Ps. 8:3-5a). Human beings are a lower order of creation than the angels.

Angels are of a higher order. This means that the incarnate Jesus, as He clothes Himself in humanity, the human nature, is, at least at this point, lower than the angels.

However, it doesn't end there. The author of Hebrews says that Jesus has "become so much better than the angels, as He has by inheritance obtained a more excellent name than they" (v. 4). Now, the author of Hebrews doesn't tell us what is the more excellent name that Jesus receives. It may be, in light of the immediate context of the passage, that the more excellent name than the angels is simply the title "Son," which is the focus of attention here. On the other hand, elsewhere in the Scriptures, we're also told of Jesus gaining a name as a result of the perfection of His obedience, and that name is not "Son" but "Lord." In Paul's letter to the Philippians, he admonishes us to have that same mind in us that was in Christ Jesus, who, even though He was in the form of God, took His equality with God not as something to be grasped or to be jealously guarded, but emptied himself (2:5-7). Obviously He did not empty Himself of His deity, but He emptied Himself of His prerogatives, of His glory, of His exaltation, and He took upon Himself the form of a man and becomes obedient as a servant, even unto death. So what Paul is saying there is, "Look at this pattern that has been given to us by Christ, who gave up the privileges that He enjoyed in heaven to condescend to our loneliness, to take upon Himself our humanity, and to bear humiliation in our stead." That's the way we should behave toward our brothers and sisters—not guarding our own status or stature, but giving it away for the benefit of others.

Paul goes on to say, "Therefore God also has highly exalted Him and given Him the name which is above every name, that at the name of Jesus every knee should bow, of those in heaven, and of those on earth, and of those under the earth, and that every tongue should confess that Jesus Christ is Lord, to the glory of God the Father" (2:9-11). This is where we see this business of the name that is attributed to Christ by God. The name that is given to Him, the name that is above every name, isn't the name *Jesus*. It is the title reserved for God in the Old Testament, the title *Adonai*, which is *Kyrios* in the New Testament. That's why the very first confession of faith of the early Christian community was simply "Jesus is Lord," reflecting the truth that God Himself has given His title to His Son.

Now that's the broader context of the elevated name. However, the immediate context of Hebrews speaks of the concept of sonship. The author uses the rhetorical question quite effectively when he says, "For to which of the angels did He ever say: 'You are my Son, today I have begotten You'? And again: 'I will be to Him a Father, and He shall be to Me a Son'?" (v. 5). In other words, God doesn't call angels "sons." Angels are servants, not sons.

In church history, these passages in Hebrews and others fueled one of the worst heresies with which the church ever had to wrestle, the Arian heresy in the fourth century, which provoked the Council of Nicea. The church was divided between the Arians, who were Unitarians, and the orthodox Christians, who were Trinitarians. Arias had an adoptionist view of Christ; he focused on the fact that Scripture calls Jesus "the only begotten Son of the Father and "the firstborn over all creation" (Col. 1:15). His point was that the word translated as "to beget" means "to be, to become, or to happen," and it is commonly used to refer to someone who has a beginning in time. So, if one is begotten, that means there was a time when he was not. Arias was saying that since the Bible says Jesus is the only begotten or the firstborn, He's obviously a creature. He may be the highest creature. He may be the first creature that God made before He made everything else. He may even be the Creator of the universe; perhaps God first made this Logos, this creature, and then gave Him the power to create the rest of the world. This is the view of Mormons and of Jehovah's Witnesses, for example. Jesus is highly exalted, but He remains a creature.

To these assertions of Arias and his followers, Athanasius and the others at the Council of Nicea said, "No." In the Nicene Creed, there is a statement that is very significant. The creed says that Christ was "begotten, not made." That is, in biblical categories, in New Testament categories, the concept of sonship is not related to biology. It's related to intimacy between the father and the son, the one who receives the blessing, the one who is the heir. That is indicated in several ways, the first of which is by Christ's being called the "only begotten." When begottenness is attributed to Jesus in the pages of the New Testament, His begottenness is singular. It is utterly unique; there are no duplicates of it anywhere in the world. So, when the Bible speaks of Christ being begotten, it speaks of begottenness in a specific sense that should lead us away from assumptions of biological generation.

In any case, the following verse says, "But when He again brings the firstborn into the world, He says, 'Let all the angels of God worship Him'" (v. 6). Again, if the firstborn of all creation is a creature, nothing could be more blasphemous than for the author of Hebrews to say, in quoting the Psalms, that all the angels should worship Him, because God prohibits the worship of creatures. But if God commands the worship of His firstborn, He is saying that the firstborn is divine and not a creature. We know that the angels are subordinate to Christ, because God commands the angels to worship Him.

The author of Hebrews continues:

> And of the angels He says: "Who makes His angels spirits and His ministers a flame of fire." But to the Son He says: "Your throne, O God, is forever and ever; a scepter of righteousness is the scepter of Your kingdom. You have loved righteousness and hated lawlessness; therefore God, Your God, has anointed You with the oil of gladness more than Your companions." And: "You, LORD, in the beginning laid the foundation of the earth, and the heavens are the work of Your hands. They will perish, but You remain; and they will all grow old like a garment; like a cloak You will fold them up, and they will be changed. But You are the same, and Your years will not fail." But to which of the angels has He ever said: "Sit at My right hand, till I make Your enemies Your footstool"? (vv. 7-13)

This passage refers to the "session" of Christ, His sitting on the right hand of God in the seat of cosmic authority. The risen and ascended Christ is given nothing less than cosmic authority as the King of kings and the Lord of lords. No angel is ever elevated to the right hand of God. In fact, no creature can ever be elevated to the right hand of God, nor would God give to any creature all authority in heaven and on earth, which authority He bestows upon His Son. This text emphasizes, as strongly as it can, the difference between angels and Jesus, the superiority of Christ over the angels.

The first chapter of Hebrews closes with these words: "Are they not all ministering spirits sent forth to minister for those who will inherit salvation?" (v. 14). Here we get a summary of the nature and the function of angels. They don't rule the cosmos, but the good angels are ministering spirits, sent forth by God. They're not sent to minister to everyone. They're sent forth to minister to the heirs of salvation, to believers. Whether we have single guardian angels or the heavenly host, such as surrounded Elisha, is a matter of continual debate. But we do have a great help.

Recently, I read a sermon by Martin Luther that I'd never read before. Luther was acutely conscious of the angelic world because of the demonic attacks he had to endure throughout his life. In the sermon, he said that if it weren't for the good angels, the angels of light who uphold the Christian church, the church would be completely destroyed by the wickedness of Satan and his minions. And so, let us remember that God has sent His good angels into the world as ministering spirits. Luther was right—our struggle is against the world, the flesh, and the Devil, and angels are there to help us as we struggle with those foes.

PART FOUR

Satan

15

The Adversary

I always feel a little bit of trepidation and apprehension when writing on the subject of Satan, that most evil of all creatures, indeed the one who is the quintessence of wickedness. I remember that when C. S. Lewis penned his famous *Screwtape Letters*, he testified afterward that he had to suffer through a period of depression while he was writing that book, for he had an acute sense that he was being oppressed by the subject about whom he was writing, namely Satan himself. Whenever I begin to talk about Satan, Lewis' testimony always provokes in me a little fear and trembling. It's one thing to consider Satan in the abstract or look at him from a strictly doctrinal position, but when we come face-to-face with the biblical teaching of Satan, who is the saints' archenemy, there is reason to proceed with great caution.

Once, when I was teaching in a college classroom, I asked the students in the class how many of them believed in the existence of God. I had thirty students in the class, and thirty students raised their hands. Then I said, "OK, how many of you believe in the existence of Satan?" Three of the students raised their hands. I was taken aback by that, and I said, "Why is it that you believe in God and not in Satan?" Their responses showed that they had put Satan in the category of witches, goblins, and things that go "bump" in the night; in other words, they had relegated Satan to the realm of superstition. I said, "If we define God as a spirit being who has the capacity to influence human beings for good, and you all affirm that, what's the problem with speaking of a spirit being who has the capacity to influence people for evil? Both are invisible, but at the same time, we have manifest evidence in history of the outbreak of unspeakable evil."

When I pressed the students about their association of Satan with superstition, one of the students said, "You surely don't believe in a little guy in a red suit who carries a pitchfork and has cloven hooves and horns, do you?" I replied that I don't believe that Satan wears a red suit and so on. That portrait of Satan dates from the Middle Ages, a time when Christian people were acutely conscious of the reality of the spirit world and particularly of the reality of Satan. They took steps to defend themselves from the wiles of Satan, and in trying to identify his weak points, they came to the conclusion that his greatest point of vulnerability was his pride. So they attacked him at that point by making silly caricatures of him in order to poke fun at him. No one in the church at that time believed that Satan actually wore a red suit, carried a pitchfork, and had hooves and horns.

What, then, do the Scriptures tell us about Satan? The name *Satan* means "adversary," and I think that's an appropriate name for him because that's what he is. He's not simply an archfiend, given to wickedness; he is the enemy of everything that is good. He is the adversary of all who put their trust in Christ; and, of course, his most despised enemy is Christ Himself. At the time of the fall, when God responded to the sin of Adam and Eve by placing curses on them, He also placed His curse on the Serpent who seduced Adam and Eve. God said that from thenceforth he would crawl on his belly and eat the dust. Then He gave the prophecy that the seed of the woman would crush the head of the Serpent, while at the same time the Serpent would bruise the heel of the seed of the woman. We call that the *protevangelium*, or the first gospel promise. This was the promise of future redemption, when the Serpent's head would be crushed. But from that moment, through the rest of redemptive history, Satan manifests himself as an adversary of the people of God.

In church history, there have been two serious distortions about the person and work of Satan. The first common distortion is to minimize his reality, or to even deny that he exists, and to fail to take him seriously as a real spiritual adversary. The second distortion is to attribute to him greater power and significance than he actually enjoys. So often the church has been influenced by dualistic perspectives that see the forces of good and evil, light and darkness, as equal and opposite powers, vying for supremacy. But the biblical view knows nothing of such a dualism, because the contest between God and Satan is no contest at all. Satan is a creature, a created being. He is always and everywhere under the sovereign power and authority of the Creator. He is in no way an equal to God Himself. As a creature, he possesses none of the incommunicable attributes of God.

When we speak of the attributes of God in theology proper, we make a distinction between communicable and incommunicable attributes. Communicable attributes are those attributes that God possesses and can communicate to us creatures to some lesser degree. For example, God, as a good being, communicates the possibility of goodness to His creatures, and we can manifest goodness—though not the perfection of goodness that is found in God. Incommunicable attributes are those attributes God possesses that not only are *not* transferred to the creature but *cannot* be transferred to the creature. One of the things that God manifestly cannot do is create another God, because as soon as God created His second god, the second god would not be eternal. He would be a creature, by definition. He would have a beginning in time from the moment the original Creator made him.

But sometimes, in our preoccupation with Satan, we are quick to assign to him attributes that belong only to God. For instance, Martin Luther warned his people about the stark reality of Satan, and he said, "Satan is as close as your own clothes." I disagree with Luther on that point. I think that when Luther was speaking of the nearness and the proximity of Satan to people, he was speaking more out of his own experience than out of his exegesis, because certainly Luther understood that Satan, as a creature, does not have the power of omnipresence or of ubiquity; that

Satan, as a creature, cannot be in more than one place at the same time. So, he can't be as close to you as your clothes and at the same time be as close to another believer as his clothes, because he can't be in those two places at the same time.

But, of course, when you have someone pop up on the screen of church history who is as critical to the advancement of the kingdom as Luther was, he very likely lived every day of his life with Satan close by, chasing him. Luther sometimes experienced what he called the *anfechtung*, the unbridled, relentless assault and attack that the prince of darkness brought against him. We can understand why Luther would have been in Satan's crosshairs—if the Devil could get Luther to fall, the Reformation might well fail.

But I think we can take some solace in the thought that it's unlikely we'll ever meet with Satan in our lifetimes. He has bigger fish to fry. He's not going to chase after the little guys. But nevertheless, he has a host of minions, his demons, to do his work for him, and so they may surround us as close as our clothes, and satanic emissaries may besiege us, and we have to be alert to that. But it's unlikely that you and I will encounter the Prince of Darkness himself. I say that because he is not omnipresent. That is an attribute that belongs only to God.

Also, he's not omniscient. Satan does not know everything. Satan is a creature, and he is defined by the limits of creatureliness. Remember, we are lower than the angels, so angels have more power than we have, presumably more knowledge than we have, and so on, but they're still far below the level of God Himself. So let's not be guilty of attributing to Satan divine characteristics. In that case, we overestimate him.

What is he actually like? The Scriptures tell us a lot about his character and his being. When he is first introduced in the earliest pages of the Bible, he is said to be more "crafty" or "subtle" than all the other beasts of the field. When he approaches Adam and Eve in their Edenic paradise, Satan comes to seduce them, and he comes with great guile. He comes to Eve with a question: "Has God indeed said, 'You shall not eat of every tree of the garden'?" (Gen. 3:1b).

In one sense, this question is absurd. God had not said they could not eat of every tree in the garden; in fact, God had said to His creatures, "Of every tree of the garden you may freely eat, but of the tree of the knowledge of good and evil you shall not eat" (Gen. 2:16b-17a). There was one exception to their freedom to eat. But Satan comes and asks, "Did He say you can't eat from all of them?" What's so subtle about that? One of Jean-Paul Sartre's arguments against the existence of God was based on the assumption of human freedom. He said that if man is truly free, God cannot exist, because as long as there's a God dictating the rules, however slight they may be, if God is sovereign, then man cannot be autonomous. To be autonomous means to be a law unto oneself, answerable to no one. The biblical view is that God is free, and He creates His creatures and gives them freedom, but their freedom is limited by God's decrees. Sartre was saying that unless you're totally free, you're not really free. Unless you're autonomous, you're not free at all. This very sophisticated philosopher in the twentieth century gave basically the same argument that the Serpent gave in the garden, because the subtlety of the suggestion was this: "Well, Eve, if God puts a restriction on this tree over here, He might just as well have said you can't eat from any of the trees in the garden."

Then Satan moves from subtlety to a direct assault. After Eve says, "We may eat the fruit of the trees of the garden; but of the fruit of the tree which is in the midst of the garden, God has said, 'You shall not eat it, nor shall you touch it, lest you die'" (vv. 2-3), Satan says, "You will not surely die. For God knows that in the day you eat of it your eyes will be opened, and you will be like God, knowing good and evil" (v. 4). The plum that was set before our original parents was not only idolatry but deification.

Satan is characteristically described in the Scriptures as a liar, and we are told that he is the father of lies (John 8:44). His entrance into redemptive history is heralded by the great lie that he spoke to Adam and Eve, which was the promise of autonomy: "If you really want to be free, if you eat of that fruit, you will be asserting your independence. You will be throwing off the yoke of this restrictive God, and you will be as God. You will be divine. You will no longer be subordinate to Him." All this was a lie, and yet every time we sin, we believe this lie, because every time we sin, we set up our own desires over the desires of God. We deny God's right to reign over us. In the slightest sin, we commit cosmic treason, because we try to overthrow the reign of God over our lives. We will not have God reign over us, and we succumb to this lie that we were given at the beginning.

So, Satan is clever and crafty. Not only that, but the Scriptures portray Satan as incredibly strong. He's no match for God. He is not omnipotent. But he is potent, and he is more potent than we are. When our Lord said that Simon Peter was going to betray Him and deny Him three times, Peter protested and said he would never do it. Jesus said: "Simon, Simon! Indeed, Satan has asked for you, that he may sift you as wheat" (Luke 22:31). Jesus was saying to Peter, "You think you're strong, but you're a piece of cake, you're duck soup to the Prince of Darkness." Satan is so much stronger than Peter was, and he is described in the New Testament as a roaring lion who goes about seeking someone he may devour (1 Pet. 5:8).

In Scripture, the lion is always the image of strength. The positive application is to the Lion of Judah, to the King who has un-opposable strength. The negative application is to Satan, a roaring lion for whom we are no match. However, as I said, Satan does not have the divine attribute of omnipotence. His power is limited, and we have an admonition in Scripture that suggests that as powerful as this lion is, his power and craft are resistible. We are told to resist him, and we are promised that if we do resist him, he will flee from us (James 4:7). So I have this image in my head of this gigantic, sinuous, muscular lion on the prowl. He approaches us and growls, and he bares his teeth. But if we resist him, his tail goes between his legs and he takes off in cowardly retreat.

At the same time, we are told that the Christian possesses a power that is not inherent to our humanity, but a power that is stronger than Satan, and it is the power of the Holy Spirit. We are told, "He who is in you is greater than he who is in the world" (1 John 4:4b). So, when we are covered with the whole armor of

God and have the indwelling Holy Spirit, we have the power to resist Satan and to overcome him.

I love to sing Luther's great hymn, "A Mighty Fortress Is Our God," which is based on Psalm 46. This song gives much attention to God as our fortress, reminding us that He is our great strength and our defense against Satan, against a world that is filled with devils that threaten to undo us. But God has given us the power of His Word, the power of the truth, the power of the Spirit, through which we can overcome these forces of hell. After Luther died, when his followers would grow discouraged, his chief disciple, Philip Melanchthon, would say, "Let's sing the forty-sixth. Let's sing 'A Mighty Fortress.'" Thus they gained new strength to resist the Devil.

16

The Angel of "Light"

One of the things that's most often overlooked about the nature of Satan is his metamorphic character. When we speak of metamorphosis, we speak of that which changes in its outward appearance. For instance, the crawling caterpillar goes through a metamorphosis to become a beautiful butterfly. What I mean in describing Satan as metamorphic is his capacity, as we say in theology, to manifest himself *subspecies boni*, which literally means "under the auspices of the good"—that far from being the ludicrous character in a red suit and carrying a pitchfork that we talked about in the last chapter, he rather has the capacity to manifest himself, as Scripture says, as an angel of light (2 Cor. 11:14). He doesn't come against us baring fangs, with a hideous visage; rather, he approaches us disguised in beauty, looking attractive. That's part of the allure of his seductive techniques. If Satan were to manifest himself in a human person, it would not be some horrible, famous, miserably wicked person like Osama bin Laden or Adolf Hitler. Rather, he would come on the stage of history looking like a saint. Satan would try to appear as someone laudable, someone who manifests some kind of righteousness, but of course he would do it in a hypocritical manner because he is a liar.

Satan is called in Scripture "the ruler of this world" (John 12:31), for that is his domain. His two main activities in the world are temptation and accusation, and it's very important to understand both of these. The one with which we're most familiar is his function as the tempter. We've already seen how, in paradise, he seduced Adam and Eve by tempting them to sin. We also know that his full powers and expertise were unleashed against Jesus in His hellish experience of temptation in the Judean wilderness. I shudder to think of what our Lord went through in that forty-day experience.

The differences between the environment in which Jesus was subjected to the power of Satan and that in which Adam and Eve were tempted are overwhelming. Adam and Eve were tempted in the midst of paradise, in a luscious garden where food was available at every point. Jesus was subjected to the assault of Satan in the midst of the Judean wilderness, one of the most desolate places on earth. The only living things there are a few birds, rabbits, scorpions, and snakes. It's a horrible place. And yet, there was Jesus, for forty days, in this place of desolation, subjected to the unbridled attack of the adversary, of Satan. Adam and Eve faced their attack on full stomachs; Jesus was assaulted after forty days of fasting, when He had the natural, biological pangs of hunger. Also, the assault came against Adam and Eve while they had the mutual strength of human companionship and fellowship. Søren Kierkegaard said that there's no more devastating condition for a human being to be subjected to for any period of time than that of solitude. If we want to punish a prisoner who is already behind bars, we put him into solitary confinement. But Jesus was utterly alone during His period of forty days, when the temptation came.

Think of Jesus' parable of the prodigal son, who behaves one way when he's in the father's house and with the family, and doesn't manifest his radical degeneration until he goes into a foreign country where he's anonymous and there is no expectation of a certain manner of behavior. Our Lord was subjected to anonymity there in the desert, and Satan tried to exploit it, saying: "Just kneel down to me. Genuflect once. No one's going to know; no one's going to see it. If you do it, all the kingdoms of the world will be Yours." This is Satan's forte: to come to the people of God and try to seduce them to sin.

Sin itself has such great attraction for us. If we know anything about the things of God, we know that sin can never make anyone happy, yet we're driven to seek our own happiness. Jonathan Edwards once said that the action of the will, the action of volition, is the mind choosing what seems to be good for us at the moment. So when we do something, we choose to do it, not because we think it has any moral righteousness to it, but because we think that it will be good for us. We get confused between happiness and pleasure. Sin brings pleasure, but never happiness. We haven't learned that yet; we won't learn it until we find our only happiness in God and in the things of God, when we enter into the heavenly state. In the meantime, we're subject to these seductive advances by Satan, who makes sin look good to us, with the promise of pleasure.

Satan tempted Adam and Eve; he tempted Jesus; he tempted Peter. He seems to go after all of the people of God in the pages of Scripture. By contrast, we are told, God never, ever tempts us (James 1:13). This is a great difference between Satan and God. However, Scripture tells us that God sometimes will put us in the place of testing. He tested Abraham by command-ing him to sacrifice Isaac. It was the Holy Spirit who led Jesus into the wilderness to be tested by Satan. Yet God never tries to encourage us to sin. This is where the story of Job is so instructive for us.

In the first chapter of Job, we read this description of him: "There was a man in the land of Uz, whose name was Job; and that man was blameless and upright, and one who feared God and shunned evil" (v. 1). What a tremendous description of integrity. He had seven sons and three daughters. He had seven thousand sheep and three thousand camels. This may have made him the richest man in the world. "His sons would go and feast in their houses, each on his appointed day, and would send and invite their three sisters to eat and drink with them" (v. 4). The family was wonderful. "So it was, when the days of feasting had run their course, that Job would send and sanctify them, and he would rise early in the morning and offer burnt offerings ac-cording to the number of them all. For Job said, 'It may be that my sons have sinned and cursed God in their hearts.' Thus Job did regularly" (v. 5). He was the paradigm of virtue as a father in Scripture.

And then what happened? What caused Job's world to cave in and disintegrate?

> There was a day when the sons of God came to present themselves before the LORD, and Satan also came among them. And the LORD said to Satan, "From where do you come?" So Satan answered the LORD and said, "From going to and fro on the earth, and from walking back and forth on it." Then the LORD said to Satan, "Have you considered My servant Job, that there is none like him on the earth, a blameless and upright man, one who fears God and shuns evil?" So Satan answered the LORD and said, "Does Job fear God for nothing? Have You not made a hedge around him, around his household, and around all that he has on every side? You have blessed the work of his hands, and his possessions have increased in the land. But now, stretch out Your hand and touch all that he has, and he will curse You to Your face!" (vv. 6-11)

This is the challenge that Satan brings to God. He's already accusing Job of hypocrisy. He's saying: "I've been all over the earth, and everyone down there is in my pocket. I'm the prince of that world. They're all following me." So God says: "What about Job? Have you seen My servant Job, who is upright and blameless?" "Ha!" Satan says. "Of course! I'm not going to look a gift horse in the mouth. You've put a hedge around him; You've given him more wealth than anyone else in the world. Does Job serve You for nothing? Of course not. But let me at him and I'll show You that Job is a fair-weather follower. When I'm finished with him, he'll curse You to Your face." So God says: "I'll take the hedge away, and we'll see what happens." That leads to this incredible story in the Old Testament of the persistent misery that Satan wrought in the life of this godly man.

This should teach us something about the activity of Satan. Satan can introduce great harm to our lives—bodily afflictions, loss of possessions, all kinds of misery. But this is where we're most tempted to separate Satan from God and to blame all of our calamities, all of our misfortunes, on Satan, as if he has a power all his own to wreak havoc in our lives. We need to see that everything that Satan does is always under the sovereign authority of God. Satan can't move a finger without divine permission.

Jesus understood this. Also, He understood the situation in which Job was placed, the situation Adam and Eve faced in the garden, and certainly He never forgot the situation He endured in the isolation of the Judean wilderness. Thus, when He taught His disciples to pray, He said, "In this manner, therefore, pray" (Matt. 6:9), after which He taught them the Lord's Prayer, which includes this line: "And do not lead us into temptation, but deliver us from the evil one" (v. 13a). There are two things about this portion of the Lord's Prayer I want to mention. The first is that it's stated in a grammatical form called parallelism, where the second line means the same thing as the first line, only in different words. Second, for the life of me, I can't understand why most English Bibles for years and centuries have translated that phrase as "deliver us from evil," where evil is spoken of in the abstract. The Greek word so often translated as "evil" here in the Lord's Prayer is *poneros*, which is more accurately translated as "evil one," as the *New King James Version* does. "*Poneros*" is a title for Satan.

So what is Jesus saying? Is He saying we should pray that God would put a hedge around us and not put us into the place where we are exposed to the assaults of Satan? That should be our prayer, knowing that we are vulnerable all the time to the enemy. We say: "God, protect us. Be our citadel. Be our mighty fortress. Protect us from the attacks of Satan." We see what happened with Job. The hedge came down and, literally, all hell broke loose in his life. His suffering was so severe and so intense that his best friends, who previously had assumed that he was a man of great integrity, came to him while he was sitting on the dung heap with his sores, saying: "Job, you must have done something really bad to be in this kind of condition, because you're the most miserable man in the world. You must have the most miserable record of sin in all the world." Even his closest companion, his wife, couldn't stand to see her husband suffer, and she said, "Give up, Job. Curse God, and die. You are going to get relief only if you will curse God." Job was saying, "Though He slay me, yet will I trust Him," but she was saying: "Stop that. You can't take any more. Curse Him and die."

But Job doesn't listen to her counsel, and Satan is defeated. God is glorified and Job himself is vindicated, as all that he has lost is restored abundantly. What a fantastic story about the power of Satan and the vindication of God's people by the Lord.

Earlier I mentioned two main activities of Satan—tempting and accusing. Satan tried to tempt Job to repudiate God, and the power of the temptation was in the pain that he brought. But not only that, he came in his favorite mode of activity for the believer. Another title for Satan in the Bible is *diabolos*, which means "accuser," and Satan is seen as the accuser of the brethren (Rev. 12:10). The accusation he brings against Job is that the only reason Job is serving God at all is in response to the prosperity that God has given him. That's not true. It's a false charge, a false accusation.

We are all familiar with the way in which Satan tempts us, but his greater work, for the Christian, is accusation, to point his finger in your face about your guilt, to take you away from the cross, away from the gospel, and point out how bad you are. The thing that's so terrible about Satan functioning as a prosecuting attorney is that he doesn't have to make up false charges. He can point out the reality of our sins and try to take away our joy, our peace, our trust in the gospel. One of the difficult things in the Christian life is to discern between the work of the Holy Spirit in convicting us of sin and the work of Satan in accusing us of sin, because they both may be pointing at the same transgression. But I've noticed this difference: When the Holy Spirit convicts us of sin, as painful as it may be for a moment, there's always something sweet in it, because in conviction, the Spirit always gives us the promise of forgiveness and restoration. However, when Satan accuses us, his purpose is to destroy us, to paralyze us, to cause us to abandon all hope. That's why Paul, when he talks about the grace of God that is so abundant and so magnificent, raises a defiant charge against Satan: "Who shall bring a charge against God's elect? It is God who justifies. Who is he who condemns?" (Rom. 8:33-34a). So when Satan comes with his accusations, we have to say: "Sticks and stones, Satan. Get out of here. We know we're guilty, but we have Christ. We have the gospel, and that is our shield against your

accusations." I love the Heidelberg Catechism's statement that Christ is our only comfort in life and death.
That's why we have to cling to Him and to the gospel,
because Satan is going to accuse us every minute.

Finally, we read in the Scriptures that Satan has an
army of assistants, the demons, and we see that their
activity was heavily concentrated during Jesus' tenure on
this earth. In fact, the very first beings to recognize the
full identity of Jesus were demons. They called Him the
Son of God and asked, "Have You come here to torment
us before the time?" (Matt. 8:29). They understood that
their days were limited. They knew there was a time
when they would be finished, but they also knew that
the time wasn't yet, and so they tried to negotiate with
Jesus. Jesus released them from inhabiting the man
they were tormenting, drove them into the pigs, and
sent them to their destruction. People ask, "Why didn't
He send them to hell?" It was simply because the time
hadn't come yet. But He dealt with them.

These demons are in many places. In the Bible, we see
them possessing people and oppressing people, causing
bodily harm, property damage, and all kinds of things.
The Christian is always faced with this question: Can
I be demon-possessed? I don't believe so. I believe that
people can be demon-possessed, but I don't think that
this is possible for a Christian, because God the Holy
Spirit resides in the regenerate person, and the Scriptures tell us, "Where the Spirit of the Lord is, there is
liberty" (2 Cor. 3:17). So, no demon can hold us hostage
to the power of Satan. Demons can oppress us, they can
harass us, they can tempt us, attack us and so on, but
thanks be to God, He who is in us is greater than he
who is in the world (1 John 4:4).

About Ligonier Ministries

Ligonier Ministries, founded in 1971 by Dr. R. C. Sproul, is an international teaching ministry that strives to help people grow in their knowledge of God and His holiness.

"We believe that when the Bible is taught clearly, God is seen in all of His majesty and holiness—hearts are conquered, minds are renewed, and communities are transformed."

Dr. Sproul

From its base near Orlando, Florida, Ligonier carries out its mission in various ways:

- By producing and broadcasting solid, in-depth teaching resources.
- By publishing and promoting books true to the historic Christian faith.
- By publishing Tabletalk, a monthly theological/ devotional magazine.
- By publishing The Reformation Study Bible.
- By training and equipping young adults, laypeople, and pastors through the Ligonier Academy of Biblical and Theological Studies.
- By producing and promoting conferences.

For more information, please visit www.ligonier.org

Christian Focus Publications
publishes books for all ages

Our mission statement –

STAYING FAITHFUL
In dependence upon God we seek to impact the world through literature faithful to His infallible Word, the Bible. Our aim is to ensure that the Lord Jesus Christ is presented as the only hope to obtain forgiveness of sin, live a useful life and look forward to heaven with Him.

REACHING OUT
Christ's last command requires us to reach out to our world with His gospel. We seek to help fulfil that by publishing books that point people towards Jesus and help them develop a Christ-like maturity. We aim to equip all levels of readers for life, work, ministry and mission.

Books in our adult range are published in three imprints:

Christian Focus contains popular works including biographies, commentaries, basic doctrine and Christian living. Our children's books are also published in this imprint.

Mentor focuses on books written at a level suitable for Bible College and seminary students, pastors, and other serious readers. The imprint includes commentaries, doctrinal studies, examination of current issues and church history.

Christian Heritage contains classic writings from the past.

Christian Focus Publications Ltd,
Geanies House, Fearn, Ross-shire,
IV20 1TW, Scotland, United Kingdom
www.christianfocus.com